SUSAN AKASS

Super Slime!

Make the perfect slime
every time with 30
fantastic recipes

CICO **kidz**

To George, for all his support.

Published in 2019 by CICO Kidz
An imprint of Ryland Peters & Small Ltd

20–21 Jockey's Fields   341 E 116th St
London WC1R 4BW   New York, NY 10029

www.rylandpeters.com

10 9 8 7 6 5 4 3 2 1

Text © Susan Akass 2019
Design, illustration, and photography
© CICO Books 2019

A CIP catalog record for this book is available from
the Library of Congress and the British Library.

ISBN: 978 1 78249 710 3

Printed in China

Editor: Caroline West
Designer: Eoghan O'Brien
Photographer: Terry Benson
Illustrator: Rachel Boulton

In-house editor: Dawn Bates
Art director: Sally Powell
Head of production: Patricia Harrington
Publishing manager: Penny Craig
Publisher: Cindy Richards

Contents

Introduction

Is it a solid? Is it a liquid? No, it's a super slime! Welcome to the wonderful world of slimes. You can stretch them, squeeze them, squelch them, bounce them, and blow bubbles in them. You can make them in wonderful colors, and add glitter, stars, and beads so they look magical. You can make them transparent, fluffy, magnetic, electric, and from many different ingredients. You will discover that they behave in all sorts of amazing and unexpected ways.

You might have heard in the media about the problem of borax in slimes and how it may cause health problems. We hope you will follow our advice on pages 18–19 to keep yourselves safe while still having fun. And for those of you who would rather not try any of the borax-based slimes, there are plenty of other projects that are completely borax-free (see page 128).

The book is divided into three chapters. **Chapter 1: Fun and Fabulous Slimes** teaches you all the basic slime recipes—some with borax, some without. **Chapter 2: Cool Activity Slimes** shows you lots of the wild and whacky things you can do with slime once you have learned how to make it. **Chapter 3: Slimes Inspired by Nature** takes you in some strange directions, using slimes in the natural world as inspiration. Following each project, there are ideas for investigations, snippets of scientific explanation, and fascinating facts to get you thinking.

At the beginning of the book, there is a section that will teach the keen scientists among you a little about the intriguing chemistry of polymers and non-Newtonian fluids. We also include a list of the ingredients and equipment you should get together for your slime workshop, tips for troubleshooting when your slime doesn't work, advice on cleaning up, and an all-important safety section on pages 18–19 which you *must* read before you get going.

The Science of Slime

Slimes are awesome, fascinating, weird… but what are they? There are two main areas of science that will help you begin to understand what is happening when you make and play with slime—the first is to do with the chemistry of polymers and the second the physics of non-Newtonian fluids. You don't need to know about either of these to have fun, but if you like science and want to impress your teachers, read on.

Magnificent molecules—the science of polymers

All the slimes in this book, plus wood, hair, elastic bands, computer keyboards, Styrofoam cups, Lego bricks, spectacles (in fact, anything plastic) are made from polymers. But what is a polymer? To explain, we have to start at the beginning, with atoms.

Everything in the universe is made out of atoms. Atoms are unbelievably small and come in over 100 different forms called elements. You will know the names of many elements already: oxygen, hydrogen, iron, gold, silver, copper, chlorine, and carbon are just a few of them. (You can find all the names of the elements in a special chart called the Periodic Table, which is the starting point for all chemistry.) Each element has a letter or letters as its symbol—for example, O stands for oxygen, H for hydrogen, and Na for sodium (from a Latin word *natrium*).

Atoms don't tend to remain single. They join together, either with atoms of the same element or with atoms of different elements, and when they do this they usually form into molecules. There are billions of different ways that elements can combine to make the molecules which are the building blocks of all the billions of different types of materials in the world (including all the different tissues which make up your body).

Molecules are written down in a code with letters standing for the atoms. Scientists make models of how the atoms join together.

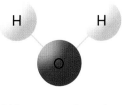

Water molecule

For example:

Water is H$_2$O
= 2 hydrogen (H) atoms + 1 oxygen (O) atom

Baking soda (bicarbonate of soda) is NaHCO$_3$
= 1 sodium (Na) atom + 1 hydrogen (H) atom + 1 carbon (C) atom + 3 oxygen (O) atoms

These two molecules are simple and easy to understand. Most of the other molecules mentioned in this book are polymers, which are much more complicated. The word "polymer" comes from two Greek words, *poly* and *meros*, which means "many parts." Polymers are made of many, many special small, repeating, molecular building blocks called monomers, which join together in long chains—like a repeating pattern of beads in a necklace. There can be hundreds of thousands or even millions of monomers in one polymer chain. Some of these polymers are natural, while some (like plastic) are man-made.

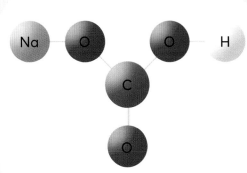

Baking soda molecule

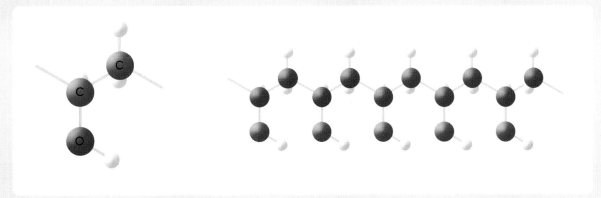

Here is the monomer for PVA (polyvinyl acetate) and then part of a chain of monomers. You will have to imagine the chain of thousands of monomers that make up the polymer.

Since polymers are very, very long chains, things happen to them that don't happen to other molecules. For instance, they can get tangled up; they can be curled up and then straighten out; they can stick to each other side by side; and when they move they can only slide over each other very slowly. This makes them really interesting because it affects how the material which they form behaves—for instance, how stretchy it is, how strong it is, and how much it bounces when you drop it. You will get to think about these behaviors when you try out the slime projects.

Not all the projects in the book involve making slime, but all of them do have something to do with polymers. Have fun getting stuck in and try to think about how the polymers in slimes make them behave.

Solids, liquids, gases... and slimes—the science of non-Newtonian fluids

Let's go back to the question we asked in the Introduction—is slime a liquid or is it a solid? Sir Isaac Newton, a very famous scientist who lived in England in the 17th century, worked out the differences between solids, liquids, and gases from the way they behaved. Here is what Newton said, among other things, about them.

Solids

✱ *A solid keeps its shape unless you bang or cut it, or apply some other force to it, in which case it becomes a new shape that it keeps.*

✱ *Even though substances made from tiny particles such as sugar, salt, and sand can be poured, they are all solids because each particle keeps the same shape and size. If you pour some salt into a cup, for example, it will make a pile in the center—it doesn't spread out to fill the shape of the cup.*

✱ *The molecules in a solid are held together tightly and cannot move. That's why a solid keeps its shape.*

Liquids

∗ A liquid can flow or be poured from one container to another. It will run out of your hand if you try to hold it.

∗ A liquid will take the shape of the container into which it is poured. The surface of a liquid always becomes flat and horizontal, although this might take some time for a very viscous (thick) liquid.

∗ The molecules in a liquid are not as tightly packed together as they are in a solid, and can move and slide past each other. That's why a liquid will take the shape of its container.

Gases

∗ Solids and liquids can be transparent, but are never invisible. Many gases are invisible, although they also come in all kinds of colors. Air is a mixture of different invisible gases.

∗ Gases do not keep their shape and don't always take up the same amount of space. They spread out and change their shape and volume to fill up whatever container they are in. If the container isn't sealed, then the gas will escape from it.

∗ Gas molecules move about freely and have a lot of empty space between them. This means they can be compressed easily (squashed into a smaller space).

Slimes

So what about slimes? Well, there are different types of slime in this book and you will quickly discover that some of them obey some of the rules of solids and some of liquids—they are neither one thing nor the other. Because they don't stick to Newton's rules they are called **non-Newtonian fluids**.

Slime made from cornstarch (cornflour) is the best place to begin to understand this. So get started by making some *Basic Cornstarch Slime* (see pages 26–29) and reading the *Inside the Science* that goes with it.

Apply force to cornstarch slime by thumping it and the mixture becomes much more viscous (thicker) and feels like a solid. Quicksand works in the same way. It hardens when you apply a force to it, which makes it difficult to escape from. These are called shear-thickening liquids.

However, some liquids become runnier when you apply a force. Tomato ketchup is a good example of one of these liquids. It is almost solid when it collects at the bottom of the

bottle, but if you shake or squeeze the bottle, it runs out easily. These liquids are called shear-thinning liquids. Xanthan gum, which is used in *Bubbling Witches' Brew* (see page 74) and *Natural Chia Seed Slime* (see page 110), is one of the magic ingredients that makes them behave like this.

When you make the slimes in the book, you will discover the wonderful world of things that stretch and flow and are somewhere between a solid and a liquid.

Setting Up Your Slime Workshop

Each of the slime recipes includes a list of the ingredients and equipment you will need. For some recipes you will have to buy special ingredients, but it is worth keeping a stock of basic slime ingredients for when you feel the urge to make slime!

Basic ingredients for PVA-based slimes

* Clear PVA glue (use good-quality glue— slime-makers in the US prefer Elmers)

* White PVA glue (use good-quality glue— slime-makers in the US prefer Elmers)

* Eyewash or contact lens solution (this must contain boric acid and sodium borate, so check the list of ingredients very carefully)

* Baking soda (bicarbonate of soda)

Plus:

* Food coloring

* Glitter

* Polystyrene balls, star confetti, and beads (or anything else you want to add to your slime)

* Shaving foam (not gel)

Kitchen ingredients for other slimes

* All-purpose (plain) flour

* Baking soda (bicarbonate of soda)

* Cooking oil

* Corn (golden) syrup

* Cornstarch (cornflour)

* Dish soap (washing-up liquid)

* Food coloring

* Gelatin

* Hand soap

* Milk

* Salt

Equipment and other items

* Bowls (small, medium, and large)

* Measuring cup or pitcher (jug)

* Measuring spoons (teaspoon and tablespoon)

* Microwave

* Microwave-safe bowls

* Mixing spoon

* Latex-free gloves (for handling PVA slimes if you have sensitive hands, or have cuts or rashes on your hands)

* Oven mitts (gloves)

* Paints and paintbrushes

* Pipettes/droppers (optional, but fun)

* Plastic containers with lids

* Toothpicks

* White vinegar (for cleaning up)

* Ziplock bags (for storing your slimes)

Food colorings

There are three types of food colorings: liquid, gel, and paste. They come in a range of colors and you can also mix them like paints to create your own colors.

Liquid food colors come in small bottles, which are cheap and readily available at grocery stores. Add a couple of teaspoons to your slime for great pastel colors.

Gel and paste food colorings are much stronger than liquid ones and less easily available. They come in a wider range of colors, too. Some come in squeezy tubes or bottles, and you just need to add a few drops to your slime. Some come in tiny jars. Use a toothpick or the very tip of a teaspoon dipped in the gel or paste to add a little at a time.

Getting ready and clearing up

Once you have set up your slime workshop, you can start having fun making slime—a bit like having your own science laboratory. Follow the guidelines below before starting and remember to clear up and store your slime properly once you've finished.

Slime is messy! To prevent lots of mess when making slime, work at a kitchen countertop or cover a table with a plastic tablecloth. Then, follow these simple tips:

✳ *Avoid using newspaper as a table covering, as the slime will stick to it.*

✳ *Keep slime away from carpets and soft furnishings. The kitchen is the best place for making and playing with slime.*

✳ *Wear an apron or old shirt to protect your clothes.*

✳ *Never throw slimes that fail or slime ingredients down the sink—they could block it.*

✳ *When you have finished making your slime, wash all the bowls and spoons in warm, soapy water. Soak any bowls that are sticky with glue (or candy if you've been making edible slime) in hot water.*

When slime gets everywhere...

✳ *If you get slime on a hard floor or table, it will pull up easily—just use a bigger lump of slime to pull up smaller pieces or to pull out any slime left in a bowl.*

✳ *If you get slime on clothes or in hair, carpets, or soft furnishings, white vinegar is your best friend. Use the vinegar, as follows:*

For carpets and soft furnishings
First scrape off as much of the slime as possible with a spoon, moving from the edge of the patch to the center to avoid spreading it. Pour on enough white vinegar to soak the slime (if the slime is dry, leave it to soak in for a few minutes) and then scrape it off. Work from the outside to the center. Blot the spot with a clean, damp cloth. When it is dry, vacuum.

For clothes
Do the same as for carpets, but once you've removed the slime from the clothing, rinse in warm water and then launder as usual.

For hair Soak long hair in white vinegar and then rinse and shampoo. If you have short hair, use the vinegar on a washcloth, taking care not to get any in your eyes. Rinse, then shampoo.

* *If your hands end up stained with the food coloring in your slime, there are several ways you can try to get it off. Be a scientist—and experiment!*

Wash well with soap and water Any remaining color will probably wear off in a few hours.

Use shaving foam You should have some in your slime kit. Rub the foam on the stain, then rinse.

Try baking soda (bicarbonate of soda) and white vinegar Mix together a teaspoon of baking soda and a little white vinegar. Rub this on **gently**, then rinse.

Try white, non-gel toothpaste Rub the toothpaste on your stained hands, then rinse.

Storing slime

Store slime in Ziplock bags or plastic storage containers with lids. Then, follow these simple rules on storage:

* *Air dries slime out, so squeeze out all the air from the Ziplock bags or use containers that have tight-fitting lids for storing your slime.*

* *Keep slime in the fridge to prevent bacteria growing on it.*

* *Throw slime away after one week.*

* *Throw slime away if it gets smelly or changes color.*

* *Never throw slime down the sink, as it can block drains. Instead, throw your slime in the trash can (rubbish bin).*

Safety first!

Here are some top tips for staying safe when making and playing with slime. Follow these simple precautions, and you will be able to have lots of fun exploring the wonderful world of slimes.

1. Never try eating any slime (except for the special edible ones made with candies and jello/jelly)—they would taste disgusting anyway.

2. Don't snack while you are making or playing with slime.

3. Keep all PVA slimes away from children under three years of age and also away from pets.

4. If you have any cuts on your hands, cover them with sticky plasters and wear latex-free gloves (like the ones doctors use). Always wear latex-free gloves if you have rashes such as eczema on your hands.

5. Keep slimy hands away from your eyes.

6. Wash your hands well after making and playing with slime.

7. Have a special slime-making kit for PVA slimes, which includes bowls, spoons, and measuring cups or pitchers (jugs). Don't use the ones you cook and eat with.

8. Always ask an adult before heating any ingredients to make slime.

9. Always check with an adult before you use any ingredients from the kitchen. Think of playing with PVA slimes as a treat, not an everyday activity. You can play with non-PVA slimes as much as you like.

Some slimes take time!

Some of the slimes in the book need to be left for several hours, overnight, or even a few days to work properly or for you to finish them. If you see the clock symbol, make sure you are happy to wait; otherwise make a slime that you can play with immediately!

Using activator safely

Many of the best slime recipes use PVA glue mixed with a borax-based activator. It is the borax in this activator that turns the PVA glue into wonderfully stretchy, squishy, bouncy, flowing slime. In the past, borax powder mixed with water has been used to make slime.

There are some health concerns about borax in slimes. For this reason, we recommend that you use either an eyewash or a contact lens solution which contains boric acid and sodium borate as an activator. Slimes made this way are sometimes described as borax-free; they are not, but contain only very small amounts of borax in a safe form. When using these, you will have to include some baking soda (bicarbonate of soda) in your slime as this reacts with the boric acid and sodium borate to produce the borate ions that make slime possible (see page 33). Borax cannot enter your body through your skin and if you follow our **Safety First!** tips (see opposite), you shouldn't have any problems.

Your carers will need to decide whether you can use borax-based activators to make your slimes, or whether you should stick to slimes made in a completely different way—perhaps with cornstarch (cornflour), as in the *Basic Cornstarch Slime* (see page 26), or with fiber powder in the *Fiber-Powder Slime* (see page 40). See page 128 for a full list of projects in the book that are borax-free and use different ingredients, but are just as much fun.

Troubleshooting—when PVA slimes go wrong

Remember, making slime takes practice—you may not get it quite right at first! Here are some tips if you think something has gone wrong with your slime.

My slime is too sticky. Even though the slime feels really sticky at first, if you keep stretching, folding, and kneading, it may come together. If not, put a little more activator on your hands and keep kneading. Do this until your slime feels right.

My slime is rubbery and breaks easily. You have added too much activator. Try soaking your slime in a bowl of hot water from the faucet (tap). When the water has cooled, start kneading the slime again. You may have to repeat this a few times. Most slimes will come good, but some may be beyond saving and you will have to start again.

My slime won't come together at all. Check to see that your activator contains boric acid and sodium borate. If it doesn't, then your slime won't work. Also check you have added some baking soda (bicarbonate of soda) to your mix. Your activator won't work without this.

Top eco-friendly tips

Now we know how bad plastic is for the environment, we ought to think about how we use plastic in our slimes. PVA glue biodegrades quite quickly, as do all the natural materials in the book, but some of the materials we have used do not, so try to follow these environmentally friendly tips:

* *Polystyrene beads, glitter, star confetti, and plastic toys are made of plastics that do not biodegrade, so use them sparingly and think about alternatives you could use instead.*

* *Plastic Ziplock bags are reusable, so make sure you wash them out so you can reuse them whenever you throw out an old batch of slime. Better still, store slime in reusable plastic containers which last much longer.*

* *Products such as PVA glue, eyewash, contact lens solution, and dish soap (washing-up liquid) usually come in plastic bottles. Be sure to wash and recycle these when they are empty.*

Chapter 1

Fun and Fabulous Slimes

Slime Gallery

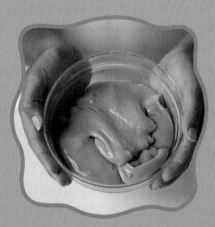

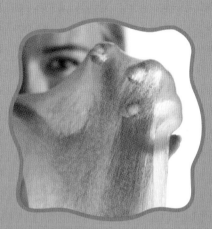

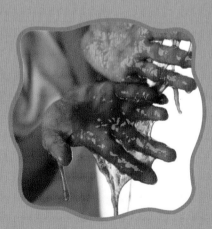

Basic Cornstarch Slime

This slime is brilliant fun to play with and will get you thinking. Is it a liquid? Is it a solid? People have filled whole swimming pools with this slime and shown that you can run across it without sinking. You need a lot of cornstarch (cornflour) for that! Start small with the quantities given for this slime and then keep scaling up if you want a large container of slime for a group of friends to play with.

You will need

10 heaping tablespoons
cornstarch (cornflour)

About 1 cup (240ml)
water

Food coloring (optional)

*

Large mixing bowl

Tablespoon

Measuring cup or pitcher
(jug)

Teaspoon (optional)

Wooden spoon

1 Add the cornstarch
to the mixing bowl.

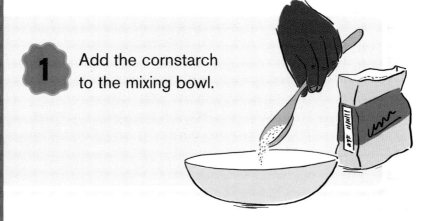

2 Pour about a quarter of
the water into the bowl
and start stirring.

3 Keep adding water, a little
at a time, and mixing until you
have a thick paste. Don't add
too much water at once. If the
mixture gets a bit too runny, add
some more cornstarch.

4 Add a little food coloring and mix it in well.

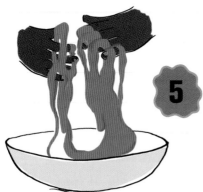

5 Slowly poke your fingers into the slime and stir them around. The slime will feel like a thick liquid, which oozes between your fingers.

6 Now punch down hard on the slime. Surprise! It feels like a solid. Squeeze a handful of the slime hard to make a solid ball. Throw the ball from hand to hand, or to someone else. Does it stay solid?

LET'S INVESTIGATE

Try adding different amounts of water. Do runnier mixes act in the same way as stiffer ones? Try using water at different temperatures. Does a warm-water mix behave differently from a cold one? Remember, to compare the effect of different temperatures scientifically, you need to have exactly the same quantities of cornstarch and water for each temperature to make it a fair test.

Inside the Science

When you mix cornstarch and water, the large, almost round, cornstarch particles can float around in the liquid. The particles are packed closely together, which makes the mixture thick, but they can still slip past each other easily. This means you can stir the mixture slowly and let it drip through your fingers like a liquid. However, if you suddenly punch or squeeze the mixture, the water quickly moves away from that place, momentarily leaving the particles packed together like a solid, before they mix with the water again to form a liquid.

Although we have described cornstarch particles as large, they are actually tiny (between one-tenth and one-thousandth of a millimeter across), but they are made up of millions of molecules.

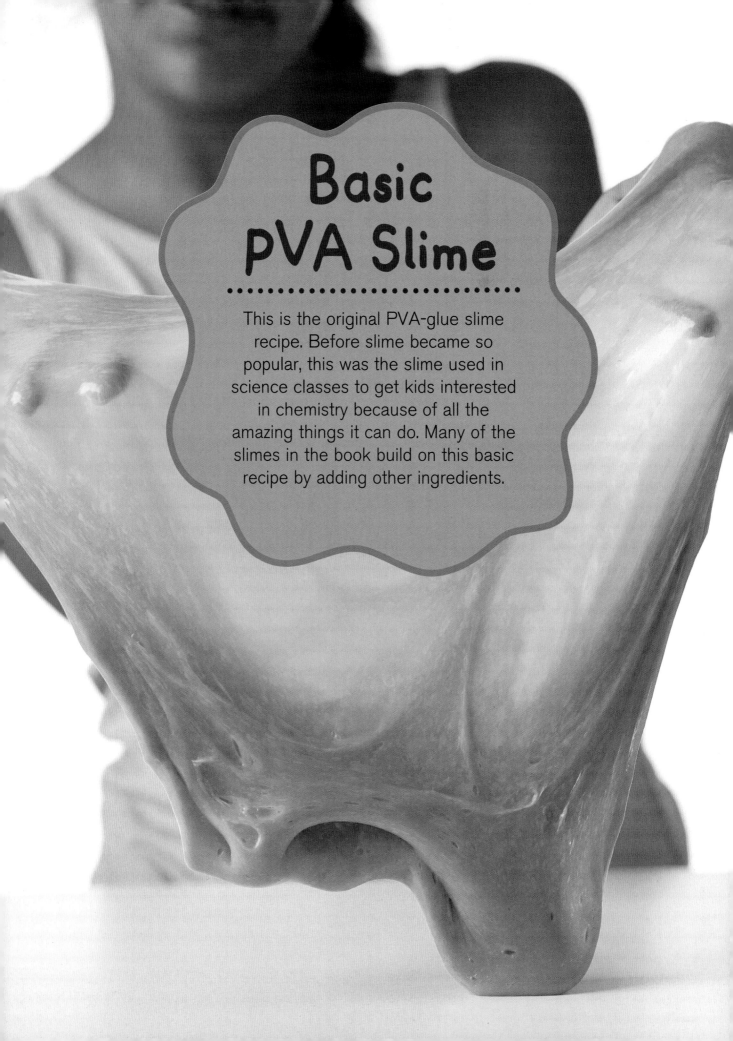

Basic PVA Slime

This is the original PVA-glue slime recipe. Before slime became so popular, this was the slime used in science classes to get kids interested in chemistry because of all the amazing things it can do. Many of the slimes in the book build on this basic recipe by adding other ingredients.

You will need

½ cup (120ml) white PVA glue

½ cup (120ml) water

½ teaspoon baking soda (bicarbonate of soda)

Food coloring (optional)

About 1 tablespoon slime activator (eyewash or contact lens solution)

Medium mixing bowl

Measuring cup or pitcher (jug)

Teaspoon

Mixing spoon

Tablespoon

Small cup

Pipette/dropper (optional, but fun)

1 Pour the PVA glue into the bowl and add the water and baking soda. Stir well until everything is thoroughly mixed together. If you wish, mix in a little food coloring, too.

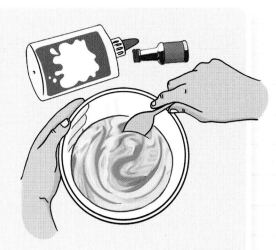

2 Pour the activator into the small cup. Use the teaspoon or a pipette/dropper to add the activator to the glue a little at a time. Keep stirring the mixture as you add the activator. The mixture will gradually get more stringy and start to come away from the sides of the bowl.

3 Continue mixing in the activator, a little at a time, until the slime reaches the consistency you want— the more activator you add, the firmer the slime will be. The more often you make slime, the better you will become at judging how much activator to use.

4 When you think the slime is ready, put a few drops of activator on your hands, then pick it up and start stretching and folding it. The slime might be a bit sticky at first, but will become soft and stretchy, and lose its stickiness, as you work it. Put a little more activator on your hands if the slime is still sticky and keep kneading it until it feels like a good slime.

5 Now start exploring what your slime can do and have a go at these experiments:

* *How far will the slime stretch?* Slowly stretch the slime between your hands until it is as long and thin as you can make it.

* *Does the slime bounce?* Roll the slime into a ball and see.

* *Does the slime flow?* Flatten the slime into a pancake and put it on top of an upside-down cup.

* *What happens if you tug the slime apart sharply?*

* *Hold a pancake of slime by its edge—what happens?*

* *What happens if you put some of the slime in a jelly mold?*

Inside the Science

The polymers (see page 8) in PVA glue can slide over each other fairly easily when the glue is liquid—although it can sometimes seem to take ages for glue to pour from the bottle! Borax activator contains borate ions (charged particles). When you add borax activator to PVA glue, the ions act as "cross-linkers," linking the long polymer molecules together and turning the long strands into a kind of net. But is the resulting slime a solid or a liquid?

This is a perfect example of a non-Newtonian fluid (see page 10). When the slime isn't being pushed or pulled, it behaves like a liquid, but when you apply a force—pulling it apart sharply or pressing it together—it behaves like a solid.

Imagine the net of molecules all tangled up, but always moving and twisting. Pull on the slime slowly and the molecules have time to become lined up next to each other, so they will slide apart—that's the slime acting like a liquid. But if you tug at the slime sharply, the molecules don't have time to line up. Instead, they end up knotted together more tightly and the slime will act like a solid.

LET'S INVESTIGATE

Try making different batches of this slime—make some that are firmer and some softer (remember, you can make your slime firmer or softer by adding more or less activator). Do they behave in different ways? Try kneading them all together at the end so you have one big lump of slime to play with.

You will need

½ cup (120ml) clear PVA glue

2 tablespoons water

½ teaspoon baking soda (bicarbonate of soda)

Food coloring and/or glitter (optional)

About 1 tablespoon slime activator (eyewash or contact lens solution)

Your choice of add-ins, such as stars or plastic fish (optional)

Medium mixing bowl

Measuring cup or pitcher (jug)

Teaspoon

Mixing spoon

Tablespoon

Small cup

Pipette/dropper (optional, but fun)

Ziplock bag

Transparent Slime

This is almost the same recipe as *Basic PVA Slime* (see page 30), but uses clear rather than white glue to get wonderful transparent slime. You can add all sorts of things to transparent slime to get exciting effects—try glitter, stars, or even little plastic fish or jewels…

1 Pour the PVA glue into the bowl and add the water and baking soda. Stir well until everything is thoroughly mixed together. Mix in a little food coloring and/or some glitter (if you wish).

2 Add the activator to the small cup. Use the teaspoon or a pipette/dropper to add the activator to the mixture a bit at a time. Keep stirring as you do this. The mixture will gradually get more stringy and start to come away from the sides of the bowl.

3 Keep mixing in the activator, a little bit at a time, until the slime reaches the consistency you want—the more activator you add, the firmer the slime will become.

4 When the slime is ready, put a few drops of activator on your hands, then pick it up and start stretching and folding it. It might be a bit sticky at first, but will become soft and stretchy, and lose its stickiness, as you work it. Put a little more activator on your hands if the slime still feels too sticky and keep kneading until it reaches the consistency you want. Knead in any stars or other small objects you want inside your slime.

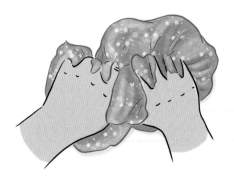

5 Hold the slime up to the light and you'll see that it isn't clear yet. Instead, it is full of bubbles, which make it cloudy. If you put the slime in a Ziplock bag and then leave it for a few days, the bubbles will gradually rise to the surface, just as they do in soda drinks, and your slime will become completely transparent.

FASCINATING FACT

A hagfish is a long, eel-like fish. When attacked by another fish, a hagfish produces a sticky, transparent slime, which clogs up the attacker's gills so that it can't breathe. The slime expands in water, and the more the attacker struggles to escape, the more the slime expands, eventually suffocating it. Sometimes the hagfish gets caught in its own slime. To get free, the hagfish ties itself in a knot and then pushes the knot down its body to scrape off the slime. Scientists have discovered that the slime has very special properties, which could be useful for making replacement tissues for human bodies or even bulletproof vests.

TOP TIP

The amount of water and activator you need to add will depend on the make of glue you use. If your slime doesn't come together easily, add some more glue and a little more activator. Remember that making slime requires you to experiment.

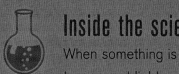

Inside the science

When something is transparent light rays pass straight through it into our eyes. But when there are lots of bubbles inside a transparent liquid, light reflects off the surface of each bubble and scatters in different directions, making it appear cloudy. Your slime is full of bubbles because they became trapped when you stirred and kneaded it. However, because your slime is a non-Newtonian fluid (see page 10), it acts like a liquid and the air bubbles are able to rise to the surface, and so it gradually becomes clear. The firmer the slime, the longer the air bubbles take to rise, and the longer it takes to become transparent.

LET'S INVESTIGATE

How long does it take for the slime to become transparent? Try making some different batches of slime—make some firmer and some softer by adding more or less activator. Which kind of slime takes the longest to clear?

Fluffy Slime

Basic slime is fun and fascinating, but if you really want to plunge your hands into slime and have a full-on slime experience, you need to make fluffy slime. This is just basic slime with shaving foam added. You can also add food coloring and glitter to make your slime even more wonderful.

You will need

1 cup (240ml) white PVA glue

¼ cup (60ml) water

1 teaspoon baking soda (bicarbonate of soda)

2–3 cups (480–720ml) shaving foam

Food coloring (in a color of your choice)

Glitter (optional)

About 2–3 tablespoons slime activator (eyewash or contact lens solution)

*

Large mixing bowl

Measuring cup or pitcher (jug)

Teaspoon

Mixing spoon

Tablespoon

1 Pour the PVA glue into the bowl and add the water and baking soda. Stir well until all the water is mixed into the glue. Squirt in the shaving foam—you don't need an exact amount, but more foam will make your slime fluffier.

2 Add a little food coloring and also glitter (if you wish) to the bowl, then mix everything together. If you need to, add some more food coloring to get just the color you want.

3 Mix in 1 tablespoon of activator. When the mixture starts to come together, begin kneading it by pulling and folding it with your hands for 5 minutes—it will feel really sticky at first.

4 Mix in another ½ tablespoon of activator and watch as the mixture turns into a wonderful, stretchy, fluffy slime. If the slime is still a bit sticky, just add more activator, a teaspoon at a time. You need to be careful, though—adding too much activator will make your slime too firm.

LET'S INVESTIGATE

Squeeze it, squish it, stretch and twist it. What can you do with fluffy slime that you can't do with *Basic PVA Slime* (see page 30)? What can you do with basic slime that you can't do with fluffy slime? Can you add more shaving foam to the mix or does that stop it behaving like slime?

Inside the Science

Foam is a strange material. It is mostly gas (95 percent) inside a small amount of liquid (5 percent), and yet it keeps its shape like a solid. When you mix foam into slime it doesn't react with the slime and it doesn't add much liquid, but it does add a lot of air. The air gets trapped (see *Blowing Slime Bubbles*, on pages 62–63) in tiny, squashy bubbles. This results in light, squishy, fluffy slime. If you keep playing with the slime, all the air will eventually escape and it will stop being fluffy.

Fiber-Powder Slime

This is a natural slime that doesn't use any borax activator. As this slime needs boiling, you should ask an adult to help you and make sure to use oven mitts (gloves) when you take the bowl out of the microwave. You'll also need to be patient and let the slime cool down first before you plunge your hands in and get all gooey.

You will need

2 cups (480ml) water

2 teaspoons fiber powder, such as Metamucil (available from grocery stores, pharmacies, and health food stores)

Food coloring (in a color of your choice)

Microwave-safe bowl and a microwave

Measuring cup or pitcher (jug)

Teaspoon

Wooden mixing spoon

Oven mitts (gloves)

1 Pour the water into the microwave-safe bowl. Mix in the fiber powder and a little food coloring. Keep mixing until the powder has completely dissolved.

2 Ask an adult to help you with the next stages. Place the bowl in the microwave and cook on a high power for about 3 minutes or until the mixture begins to boil.

3 Using the oven mitts, carefully remove the hot bowl from the microwave and stir the mixture with the wooden spoon. Return the bowl to the microwave and cook the mixture until it boils again.

4 Using the oven mitts, carefully take the bowl from the microwave and let cool. Once the mixture is cool, it will be gooey, slimy, and perfectly safe to play with.

LET'S INVESTIGATE

Most of the slimes in this book are non-Newtonian fluids (see page 10). Do you think this one is too? Experiment and find out.

Inside the Science

This natural slime is an example of a substance called mucilage, just like the mucilage found in the chia seeds in *Natural Chia Seed Slime* (see pages 110–113). The fiber powder used in this slime is ground off the outside of psyllium seeds, and so makes a smooth slime rather than the seedy chia seed slime. The long fiber-powder molecules are *hydrophyllic*, which means "water-loving." They spread out through the water to make a colorless gel that can take up more than 10 times the volume of the powder. Heating helps this process by giving the molecules more energy to move around.

Butter Slime

You will need

½ cup (120ml) white PVA glue

¼ cup (60ml) water

⅓ cup (75ml) shaving foam

¾ teaspoon baking soda (bicarbonate soda)

Food coloring (if your clay is white)

About 1 tablespoon slime activator (eyewash or contact lens solution)

2 packets Crayola Model Magic Clay (each weighing ½oz/14g)

Medium mixing bowl

Measuring cup or pitcher (jug)

Teaspoon

Mixing spoon

Tablespoon

Small cup

Pipette/dropper (optional, but fun)

This is a brilliant, smooth, non-sticky, super-stretchy slime. The magic ingredient in this slime is Crayola Model Magic Clay (not air-dry clay)—and nothing else will do. This special ingredient is not easy to find and you will probably have to order it online, but it's cool stuff that you can use for modeling, as well as making slime, so it's worth getting some.

1 Put the glue, water, shaving foam, and baking soda in the bowl. Mix everything together really well to stop the slime becoming lumpy. If you are using white clay, then add some food coloring, too.

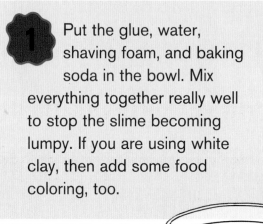

2 Add the activator to the small cup. Gradually add the activator a teaspoon or a squirt from the pipette/dropper at a time. Stir well every time you add some activator and leave the slime long enough for the activator to work. Don't add lots of activator in one go because you don't want this slime to get too firm. It still needs to be a bit wet and sticky.

3 Now it's time to add the magic ingredient—the Model Magic Clay. You need to have the same amount of clay as you have slime. If there is too much slime, take a bit out before you add the clay.

4 Knead the slime and clay together—it will take a few minutes of kneading to get the perfect result.

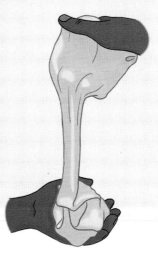

SAFETY FIRST!

Butter Slime may sound tempting, but it is not safe to eat!

LET'S INVESTIGATE

Find out just how far this slime can stretch! Does it spread like butter if you use a knife?

Dish Soap Slime

Like the putties in the *Cornstarch Challenge* (see page 56), this is another slime that uses just two simple ingredients everyone has in their home—dish soap and salt. These produce a slime that is much stickier than PVA slimes, but has good squiggle value when you let it drip down. The science behind this one is very different too.

You will need

About 1 cup (240ml) dish soap (washing-up liquid), shampoo, or liquid hand soap

Glitter (optional)

Salt, as needed

Small mixing bowl

Measuring cup or pitcher (jug)

Mixing spoon

 Pour the dish soap into the bowl and add some glitter if you want sparkly slime.

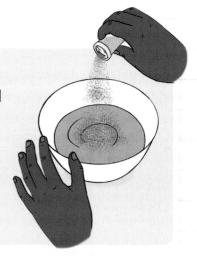

2 Sprinkle in a pinch of salt and start stirring. Keep stirring for about a minute until the dish soap begins to thicken up.

3 Sprinkle in a second pinch of salt and stir for another minute. Keep doing this until you have a good slime.

TOP TIPS

Adding too much salt will make the slime runny again. If this happens, add more dish soap and keep stirring until the mixture turns back to slime.

Never put the bowls you have used for your dish-soap experiments in a dishwasher—they will create too much foam and your dishwasher will stop working!

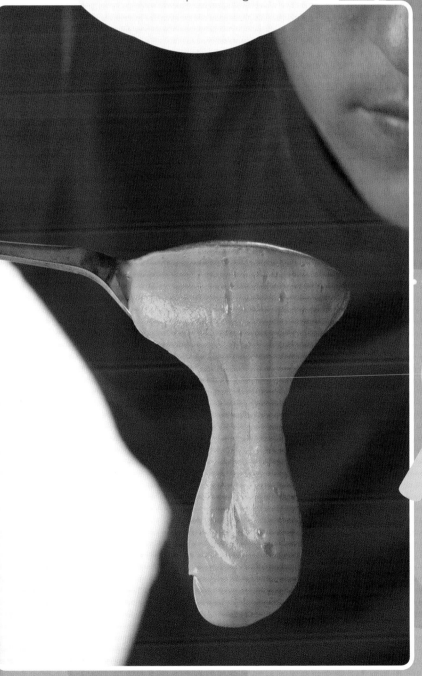

Inside the Science

Dish soap is a mixture of water and other molecules, including some called surfactants. These are long molecules with hydrophyllic heads and hydrophobic tails. *Hydrophyllic* means "water-loving" and *hydrophobic* means "water-hating." These molecules arrange themselves into balls, with the hydrophyllic heads all pointing out into the water and the hydrophobic tails all pointing away from it.

When you add salt to the dish soap, it dissolves in the water and changes the way these surfactant molecules behave—they join into bigger and differently shaped groups and the dish soap becomes a gel. If you add too much salt, then the surfactant groups break down and the mixture becomes liquid again.

LET'S INVESTIGATE

Explore what this slime can do. How firm can it get? Can you make a ball out of it? If you can, for how long will the slime hold its shape? Experiment by adding more dish soap or salt to your mixture to get the best slime you can.

Rainbow Glitter Slime

This amazing slime uses *Transparent Slime* (see page 34) as a base with lots of different colored glitters added to create a beautiful rainbow effect. You can then mix the slime into pretty swirling patterns.

You will need

½ cup (120ml) clear PVA glue

2 tablespoons water

½ teaspoon baking soda (bicarbonate of soda)

Glitter in all the colors of the rainbow (red, orange, yellow, green, light blue, dark blue, and purple)

About 1 tablespoon slime activator (eyewash or contact lens solution)

Medium mixing bowl

Measuring cup or pitcher (jug)

Teaspoon

Mixing spoon

Tablespoon

Small cup

Pipette/dropper (optional, but fun)

 1 Make a batch of *Transparent Slime* (see pages 34–37), but don't mix in any food coloring or add-ins. You also need to finish making your see-through slime before adding any glitter—this slime uses lots of glitter for more sparkly fun.

 2 Take about 1 tablespoon of the transparent slime, put it onto the countertop, and mix in 1 teaspoon of red glitter. Use your fingers to knead the glitter into the slime until it is well mixed, and set aside.

 3 Repeat Step 2 for the remaining colors of the rainbow—orange, yellow, green, light blue, dark blue, and purple. It doesn't really matter which colors you use or in what order!

4 Line up all your blobs of glittery slime, so they are just about touching each other. Pinch the blobs together with your fingers and thumb to make one long strip of slime.

5 Hold the strip of slime at each end and slowly lift it up from the countertop, so it stretches into a beautiful, glittery, rainbow-colored sheet.

6 Now let the sheet of slime go and gather it into one big lump. Twist the slime around gently so the colors swirl and flow together.

LET'S INVESTIGATE

How long can you keep the colors of the rainbow slime separate before they all blend together? What color does your slime end up?

Inside the Science

Do you remember the colors of the rainbow—red, orange, yellow, green, blue, indigo, violet? You can check them on a sunny day by putting your fingers over the end of a squirting garden hose to make a fine spray. Stand with your back to the sun and look for the rainbow. White light (normal light) is a mixture of all the colors of the rainbow. The tiny water drops from the hose split the colors, just as raindrops do when you see a rainbow in the sky.

Everything around us looks colored because each object absorbs (sucks in) all the colors of white light except the one you see and that is reflected back into your eyes. A white object reflects back all the colors of the rainbow and a black object absorbs them all, while a green object absorbs all the colors except green, a red object absorbs all the colors except red, and so on. That's how we see the colors in the slime. The glitter makes the slime sparkle because it is made of tiny pieces of plastic that are like little mirrors and reflect the light straight back to your eye. It will sparkle more in a bright light.

Crunchy Slime

The best thing about slime is how it feels between your fingers when you squish and squeeze it. If you have had fun playing with *Fluffy Slime* (see page 38), try adding some crunch! Crunchy slime is made in the same way as fluffy slime, but little polystyrene balls are added before the activator. You could also make the slime crunchy by adding snipped-up, plastic drinking straws or little beads.

You will need

1 cup (240ml) white PVA glue

¼ cup (60ml) water

1 teaspoon baking soda (bicarbonate of soda)

2–3 cups (480–720ml) shaving foam

2–3 handfuls of tiny, multicolored polystyrene balls

About 2–3 tablespoons slime activator (eyewash or contact lens solution)

*

Large mixing bowl

Measuring cup or pitcher (jug)

Teaspoon

Mixing spoon

Tablespoon

SAFETY FIRST!

Polystyrene balls are so light that it is possible to breathe them in. Store them carefully in a sealed bag and be sure to keep them away from young children.

This slime looks great left white with multicolored balls, but be careful—although it looks a bit like cake frosting (icing), it isn't safe to eat!

1 Add the PVA glue, water, and baking soda to the bowl and stir until everything is thoroughly mixed together.

2 Squirt in the shaving foam and add the polystyrene balls, then mix everything together really well.

3 Add 1 tablespoon of activator to the mixture and start stirring. When the mixture becomes gloopy and starts coming together, use your hands to stretch, fold, and pull it for 5 minutes—it will be very sticky to start with.

4 Add another ½ tablespoon of activator and keep stirring—the mixture will transform into a stretchy, crunchy slime. Add more activator, a teaspoon at a time, if the slime still feels sticky. Remember to add the activator in tiny amounts—if you add too much, your slime may be too stiff to play with.

TOP TIP

Polystyrene is a polymer that does not biodegrade (see page 8) and cannot be recycled, making it bad for the environment. We've included this project because of the interesting science behind it, but you may want to use a non-plastic alternative to add crunch—something that isn't plastic and yet won't absorb water from the slime! Try experimenting (jumbo oats work quite well), but remember food products will go bad, so if you add any, keep the slime in the fridge and throw it away after a day or two.

LET'S INVESTIGATE

Does adding polystyrene balls make the slime weaker? Does the slime break more easily when you stretch it because of the balls? What happens to the balls when you stretch the slime thinly or let it run down the sides of an upturned bowl? If you leave the slime overnight in a Ziplock bag, what happens to the balls? Predict whether they will all end up at the top or the bottom of the slime, then have a go and find out. Try this investigation with other small objects—perhaps an elastic band, small coin, paper clip, or matchstick. Find out if these objects float in water, then mix them into a batch of crunchy slime and leave this overnight. Do the same objects that float in water float in slime?

Inside the Science

The colorful balls in this slime are made from a material called polystyrene. This is another kind of polymer—a long molecule with a repeating pattern (see page 8). Polystyrene is incredibly light because it is made up of a net of molecules that are puffed full of air, whereas slime is made of a similar net of molecules that is full of water, which means it is much heavier.

You could also compare polystyrene to shaving foam. Polystyrene is mostly air bubbles contained by a solid, whereas shaving foam is mostly air bubbles contained by a liquid. The polystyrene balls rise to the surface of the slime if you leave it overnight because they float on the liquid slime as they would in water. What happened to the other objects you explored in *Let's Investigate*?

Unicorn Slime

You will need

For each slime color:

¼ cup (60ml) white or clear PVA glue

1 tablespoon water

¼ teaspoon baking soda (bicarbonate of soda)

About 2 cups (480ml) shaving foam

Food coloring (in a color of your choice)

Glitter (in a color of your choice)

About 1 tablespoon slime activator (eyewash or contact lens solution)

*

Large mixing bowl

Measuring cup or pitcher (jug)

Teaspoon

Mixing spoon

Tablespoon

Small cup

Pipette/dropper

A book about slime wouldn't be complete without unicorn slime because everybody loves unicorns and this slime seems to be everyone's favorite. This isn't really a new slime at all—just a bigger quantity of *Fluffy Slime* (see page 38) in three or more glittery colors to help create a bit of unicorn magic. You'll need to follow the recipe three or four times, but add a different food coloring each time. This is a great slime to make with friends because there will be plenty for everyone. It does use a lot of shaving foam, so be sure to have a couple of cans at hand before you begin!

1 Pour the PVA glue into the bowl and add the water and baking soda. Stir well until all the water is mixed in.

2 Squirt in the shaving foam and add just enough food coloring to make a pretty pastel color. Add some glitter for sparkle and mix everything together.

3 Measure 1 tablespoon of activator into the small cup. Use the pipette/dropper to begin adding the activator to the mixture a squirt at a time and keep stirring in the activator until the mixture starts to come together. Knead the mixture with your hands for 5 minutes—it will feel very sticky at first.

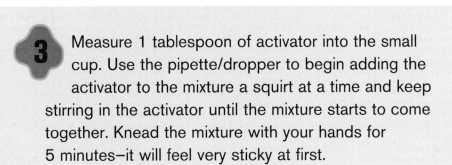

4 Add the rest of the activator, bit by bit, and watch as the mixture turns into a wonderful, stretchy, fluffy slime. If the slime is still sticky, add more activator, a squirt at a time, but be careful not to add too much in one go or it will be too firm.

5 Put the first slime to one side and begin again. Follow the instructions for Steps 1 to 4 to make three or four more slimes, but use a different color each time.

6 Stretch out all your slimes side by side and then twist them together to make magical patterns.

SAFETY FIRST!

Unicorn slime looks just like ice cream. Don't let small children eat it!

LET'S INVESTIGATE

This slime isn't about investigation or science—it's all about having lots of fun with friends and using your imagination to create a bit of magic. Enjoy!

Cornstarch Challenge

You can have awesome fun with *Basic Cornstarch Slime* (see page 26), a simple mixture of cornstarch (cornflour) and water. This challenge will get your chemistry skills working, as you have to mix cornstarch with different liquids such as dish soap (washing-up liquid) and hair conditioner. You can use anything that you would happily put on your skin or in your mouth. Make different putties and compare them! Remember to ask for permission first before you use any liquid cosmetics—they may be expensive!

You will need

Selection of different liquids (such as dish soap/washing-up liquid, hair conditioner, hand cream, yogurt, and cooking oil)

Food colorings in different colors (optional)

Cornstarch (cornflour)

*

Small mixing bowl

Tablespoon

Mixing spoon

1 Begin with the dish soap. Mix 1½ tablespoons of the soap with 2 tablespoons of cornstarch in the bowl. Use the mixing spoon until it gets too difficult to mix and then just use your hands.

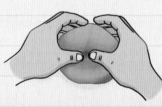

2 Knead the mixture into a soft putty. Your dish soap will probably be colored, and this will add some color to the putty. If not, then add a little food coloring.

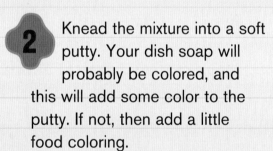

3 Now experiment! Does the slime stretch? Does it crumble? What happens when you hold the slime up—does it flow down? Try making the slime softer or firmer by adding more dish soap or more cornstarch.

4 Repeat Steps 1 and 2 with another one of your liquids, perhaps some hair conditioner or hand cream. Make the slime in another color by adding a different food coloring. Does this slime behave in the same way as the first one or is it stretchier, for example? Does this slime flow more? Is it more or less crumbly?

5 Keep experimenting with your other liquids to make a whole batch of different putties (in various colors if you wish).

LET'S INVESTIGATE

This whole project is about investigation. Now try and think of any patterns you have found out—which kinds of liquids make the best putties? Did you find that you couldn't make a putty with any of your liquids?

Inside the Science

We have discovered that water mixes with cornstarch to make a non-Newtonian fluid (see page 10). Most of the liquids you have tried in this challenge contain water, which mixes with the cornstarch. They also contain some oil or soap, which binds the slime into a putty and, as we have seen, soap molecules can behave in strange ways (see page 45).

chapter

2

Cool
Activity
Slimes

Slime Gallery

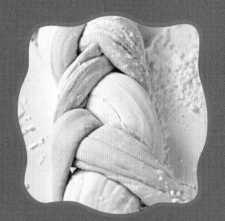

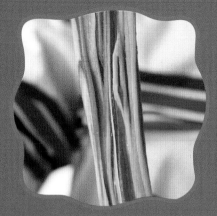

Blowing Slime Bubbles

This is a fun activity if you've already made a batch of *Transparent Slime* (see page 34), or you can just make a new batch. It would also work with *Basic PVA Slime* (see page 30), but the bubbles will be less transparent.
Have a competition to see who can blow the biggest bubbles. You need a good stretchy slime for this one.

You will need

½ cup (120ml) clear PVA glue

2 tablespoons water

½ teaspoon baking soda (bicarbonate of soda)

Food coloring (optional)

About 1 tablespoon slime activator (eyewash or contact lens solution)

*

Medium mixing bowl

Measuring cup or pitcher (jug)

Tablespoon

Teaspoon

Mixing spoon

Small cup

Pipette/dropper (optional, but fun)

Shallow bowl (optional)

Drinking straws (ideally, non-plastic)

1 Make a batch of *Transparent Slime* (see pages 34–37), but don't mix in any glitter or add-ins—just add a little food coloring if you would like colored bubbles. This slime needs to be very stretchy for you to be able to blow bubbles with it, so take it out of the bowl at an early stage, before you start stretching and kneading it.

2 Gather your slime into a blob on the countertop or in a shallow bowl. Push a straw into the slime and blow. Try blowing with the straw held in different positions—for example, deep, shallow, straight down, and at an angle. Can you blow a huge bubble?

3 Now take a small blob of slime and mold it around the end of a straw. Blow gently. How big a bubble can you make? Can you take the bubble off the straw?

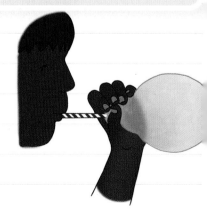

4 Another way of making bubbles is just by trapping air. Put a roll of slime on the countertop, slowly stretch it out into a really thin sheet, and then flip it back over to trap the air in a big bubble. This takes practice. From there, you could go on and try making a giant bubble. Make a much bigger quantity of slime and ask one or two friends to help you. You'll need a hard, smooth kitchen floor to do this, rather than the countertop. Flatten the slime into a pancake and hold it at the edges with your friends' help. Lift the pancake up and down (as you would a parachute in parachute games). The slime will stretch and stretch into an enormous bubble—after about three lifts, bring it right down onto the floor and try to trap the air inside the bubble.

Inside the Science

These bubbles are complicated. When you blow into the slime you force air into it. The air can't escape, and so the slime stretches to make an air pocket or bubble. At first, the slime behaves like a solid and the bubble is a bit like a balloon. The elastic slime is trying to pull back, so the inside is under high pressure. Then the slime begins to act like a liquid, flowing around the air, so it is more like a bubble. Look at a big soap bubble and you'll see the soap moving around in it.

LET'S INVESTIGATE

If you are making any of the other slimes in the book, try blowing bubbles with them. Which slimes make the best bubbles? Can you predict before you begin experimenting?

Magnetic Slime

This black magnetic slime is super-cool. You can use a magnet to pull it up into peaks and make it creep along a surface. But be careful—iron oxide is very black and you can get really messy when you play with it (although it will wash out of your clothes). Mix this slime with some silver or black glitter for a more metallic effect.

You will need

½ cup (120ml) white PVA glue

½ cup (120ml) water

½ teaspoon baking soda (bicarbonate of soda)

2–3 tablespoons black iron-oxide powder (magnetite) or iron filings (available from hardware stores or online)

Glitter (optional)

About 1 cup (240ml) shaving foam

About 1 tablespoon slime activator (eyewash or contact lens solution)

Strong magnet

✳

Medium mixing bowl

Measuring cup or pitcher (jug)

Teaspoon

Mixing tool

Tablespoon

Ziplock bag (if you are using iron filings)

SAFETY FIRST!

Today you can get super-strong magnets called neodymium magnets. You need to be very careful with these, especially if you have a pair of them, as they can click together with such force that they trap your skin and give you a blood blister. They can also damage electronics— so, when we say that you need a strong magnet, don't get one that is too strong and always take care.

1 Pour the PVA glue into the bowl and add the water and baking soda. Stir well until everything is thoroughly mixed together.

2 Mix in the iron-oxide powder until the glue is completely gray all the way through—it will turn black after a while. Add some glitter, if you wish. If you use iron filings, they won't color the glue in the same way.

3 Mix in the shaving foam until you have a soft, fluffy slime.

4 Mix in ½ tablespoon of activator. When the mixture starts to come away from the sides of the bowl, knead it with your hands for 5 minutes—it will be very sticky at first. Add another teaspoon of activator and keep kneading. If the mixture is still sticky, add more activator, a teaspoon at a time. Try not to make the mixture too stiff—the looser it is, the more easily it will move toward the magnet.

5 If you are using iron filings, put your magnet inside a Ziplock bag and zip it up. Slowly bring your magnet toward the slime and watch it begin to move. Hold the magnet very slightly away from the slime and see a long, slimy tentacle begin to grow. Keep moving the magnet away from the slime to make the tentacle grow longer.

6 Now try holding the magnet above the slime until a spike is pulled up toward the magnet. How tall can you make the spike of slime grow?

TOP TIP

If you are using iron filings, putting the magnet inside a plastic bag will stop the iron filings sticking to the magnet—when this happens, they are impossible to get off. Instead, the iron filings will stick to the plastic and fall off as soon as you remove the magnet from the bag.

LET'S INVESTIGATE

Try making slime mixtures with different amounts of shaving foam and activator. Which combination allows the magnet to pull the slime most easily?

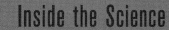

Inside the Science

The black powder used in this slime is a kind of iron oxide (often called ferrous oxide). This can be found naturally as a rock called magnetite and is always magnetic. The powder is used as a black dye, which is why it makes such a great black slime. The more iron oxide you add, the more magnetic the slime will be. But the slime will also be stiffer—and the stiffer the slime, the less it can move toward the magnet.

Super-Bouncy Glitter Balls

Playing with slime involves lots of stretching, squishing, and squashing. Although slime does bounce, it doesn't bounce that well. For this slime project, it is the bounciness that matters, so you make it in a slightly different way.

You will need

2–3 tablespoons slime activator (eyewash or contact lens solution), depending on the size of bowl

½ teaspoon baking soda (bicarbonate of soda)

About 2 tablespoons clear PVA glue

Glitter (in a color of your choice)

✱

Small mixing bowl

Teaspoon

Tablespoon

Mixing spoon

1 Add the activator and baking soda to the bowl until it is about ½in. (1cm) deep. Slowly pour the glue into the activator. How much glue you need will depend on the size of ball you want to make, but about 2 tablespoons makes a nice-sized ball. Sprinkle in a little glitter at this stage, too, and mix everything together.

2 The glue will begin to harden as soon as it hits the activator. This is fine because you need this slime to be much firmer than usual. Take the slime out of the bowl, and squeeze, squash, and roll it in your hands until you have a perfect glittery, bouncy ball.

3 If your slime is still quite stretchy, put some activator on your hands and work it in. The firmer the slime, the bouncier the ball will be. But make sure you don't add too much activator, or the slime will begin to crack and crumble. You may need to mix a few batches of slime until you get it just right. You'll be able to make another bouncy ball with the activator left in the bowl.

LET'S INVESTIGATE

How many times does your slime ball bounce when you drop it? How high can it bounce? Does the ball bounce higher on different surfaces?

Inside the Science

This slime contains more borax activator than basic slime, so there are more cross-links between the polymers, which produces a very firm slime. However, this is still one of those non-Newtonian liquids (see page 10). Leave the ball alone and the slime will flow, slowly flattening into a pancake, although it won't roll together again as easily as stretchy slime. When you move any slime quickly it becomes elastic, pulling back hard against you when you try to stretch it until it reaches a point where it breaks. The more cross-links there are in the slime, the more elastic it becomes. The more elastic a ball is, the better it bounces when it hits the ground (see page 93).

Nebula in a Jar

Have you ever seen any of the breathtaking images of space nebulae? Find some images on the Internet to see just how beautiful they are. Nebulae are vast clouds of dust and gases deep in space, which shine with colored light. This nebula in a jar recreates the wonderful effect of light, color, and sparkle swirling together, especially if you place it on a sunny windowsill or in front of a lamp in a dark room. It has one very strange ingredient—a diaper (nappy)!

You will need

Food colorings (in colors such as red, purple, deep blue, turquoise, and yellow)

Water

Disposable diaper (nappy)

Glitter (in a color or colors of your choice)

Star confetti

*

About 5 plastic cups

Measuring cup or pitcher (jug)

Mixing spoon

Large plastic container

Large glass jar with a lid (a preserving jar with a glass lid, such as a Kilner or Mason jar, works well)

Bamboo skewer

1 Decide on the colors for your nebula. Red, purple, deep blue, and turquoise, with perhaps a dash of yellow, work really well. Use a plastic cup for each color and mix about a ⅓ cup (75ml) of water—that's about 5 tablespoons—with food coloring to create your colors. You may need to mix different colors together to get the exact ones you want and you can also make some stronger than others.

2 Spread out the diaper in the plastic container and pour over 2–3 cups (480–720ml) of water. Leave for a few seconds for the diaper to soak up the water.

3 Gently tear away the top layer of the diaper to reveal the loose lumpy material inside. This is what you need for your nebula. Scrape all this loose material into the plastic container. Add another cup or two (about 240–480ml) of water and watch the material swell and become more like pieces of clear jelly.

4 Spoon some of this jelly into the jar to make a layer at the bottom. The thickness of the layer depends on how much of the first color you want in the jar. Don't flatten down the material, but leave it in hills and valleys.

5 Pour over the first colour of your nebula—it will be absorbed by the jelly. Sprinkle some glitter and star confetti around the inside of the jar. These won't show up in the middle, so don't waste any by putting them there. Push the glitter and confetti down the inside of the jar with the skewer or a spoon.

6 Add more jelly and another nebula color, then push down more glitter and star confetti. Keep building up the layers of colored material and pushing down the glitter and confetti around the inside of the jar.

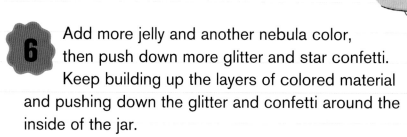

7 Use a spoon to push the layers down in some places, so there are dips and waves in the colors. When the jar is full, put on the lid and admire your galactic creation.

FASCINATING FACTS

When you pulled the diaper (nappy) apart you will have noticed how much plastic and other material, as well as super-absorbent polymer, makes up a disposable diaper. A baby will use about 500 diapers before he or she is potty trained—that's enough to fill 130 black trash (rubbish) bags. In the United States, about 20 billion diapers are thrown into the trash each year—you can work out how many bags they would fill. As a diaper takes about 500 years to biodegrade (see page 21), disposable diapers are obviously a big environmental problem. It is difficult to persuade parents and carers not to use them when they are so easy and efficient, but eco-friendly alternatives are available.

Inside the Science

We have included this activity because the powder inside the diaper is another example of a polymer (see page 8). This polymer is super-absorbent. There are fibers mixed with the powder that spread out the polymer and the liquid it absorbs so the baby doesn't end up sitting on a squishy lump of gel when it wees. Babies used to get sore bottoms because they were often wet. Now that they wear polymer diapers, they are much more comfortable.

LET'S INVESTIGATE

Take another diaper and put it in a dry plastic container. Don't wet the diaper this time, but tear it open and pull out all the loose material. This will be fluffy and more like absorbent cotton/cotton wool because it is dry. Put all this fluffy material in a Ziplock bag. Any powder that escapes from the diaper into the container is important, so pour this into the bag, too. Blow into the bag to inflate it a little and then seal it. Now shake the bag around and flap it against a tabletop. The powder will be shaken out of the cotton-like fibers into the bottom of the bag. Pull the fluff out of the bag and pour the powder into a clear glass or plastic cup. Add about ½ cup (120ml) of water and stir. The powder will expand to form a firm gel—feel it with your finger and try turning the cup upside down. That's what holds the wee in a diaper!

Bubbling Witches' Brew

You will need

About 2 cups (480ml) white vinegar

1¼ teaspoons xanthan gum

Liquid food colorings

3–4 tablespoons baking soda (bicarbonate of soda)

Glitters

Small mixing bowl

Large mixing bowl

Measuring cup or pitcher (jug)

Teaspoon

Mixing spoon

Tablespoon

Pipette/dropper (optional, but fun)

Bamboo skewer

Safety goggles (optional)

Make this concoction the center of a Hallowe'en party. Pour on the goo and see the bubbles slowly grow and break through. Add colors and glitters, and swirl them together as you chant your magic spells. Use dark, mysterious colors and dark glitters for witches or bright magical colors for a fairy spell.

1 A few hours before your party, mix the vinegar and xanthan gum together in the small bowl. The gum will clump together to form lumps, but this doesn't matter. Add a little food coloring.

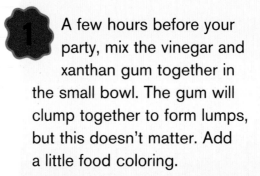

2 Place the mixture in the fridge to thicken up into a slimy goo.

3 When you are ready to make your bubbling brew, put a thick layer of baking soda at the bottom of the large bowl.

Carefully spoon the xanthan gum mixture over the top. Don't stir, but wait for the bubbling to begin!

Take turns adding either a small squirt or teaspoon of food coloring or a pinch of glitter to different places on top of the goo and watch how these spread out over the surface.

6 Use the bamboo skewer to cut gently through the gooey mixture so that the colors begin to blend, but don't stir or the mixture will foam rather than bubble. Cutting the goo like this will make it bubble more when it slows down, as will gently shaking the bowl.

Stand back and watch the bubbles of carbon dioxide as they fizz and erupt from the brew. If you want to look at the eruptions more closely, wear safety goggles to protect your eyes.

When the mixture has nearly stopped bubbling, you can stir everything together and it will froth up into a soft, slimy foam!

LET'S INVESTIGATE

Make a xanthan gum mixture with a different viscosity (thickness). Which one works best—that's a matter of opinion, not science!

FASCINATING FACT

Xanthan gum is found in lots of different foods, such as ice cream, and in domestic products like toothpaste. It makes liquids more viscous (thicker and less runny). Xanthan gum also makes liquids act in a non-Newtonian way (see page 10). For instance, it holds all the ingredients together in salad dressing in a fairly thick mixture, but when you shake the bottle, the dressing becomes much more runny and pours out easily. On the salad, where there is no shaking going on, the dressing becomes thick again and clings to the leaves.

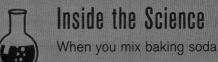 Inside the Science

When you mix baking soda and acid, a chemical reaction takes place that produces the gas carbon dioxide. Vinegar contains an acid called acetic acid. When you spoon the vinegar and xanthan gum mixture on top of the baking soda, the reaction begins and carbon dioxide bubbles force themselves up through the thick goo. Bubbles can escape very quickly from water because water molecules move around easily. The xanthan gum slime is much more viscous (thicker) than water because— you guessed it—it is another polymer. This means the bubbles rise to the top slowly and have more time to grow before they float away from the source of the gas (the reacting baking soda and vinegar) which is making them bigger.

Electric Slime

This is a really quick and easy activity, but it is very dramatic, too. Watch how the power of static electricity can make electric slime move. You only need small quantities of slime for this one.

1 Put the cornstarch in the cup or bowl. Gradually add 1 tablespoon of cooking oil, stirring all the time with a mixing spoon, to make a thick liquid slime that drips slowly off the spoon.

2 Blow up the balloon and rub it on your hair to charge it with static electricity.

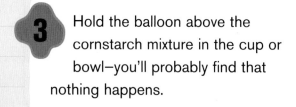

3 Hold the balloon above the cornstarch mixture in the cup or bowl—you'll probably find that nothing happens.

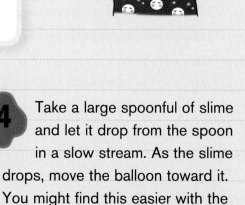

4 Take a large spoonful of slime and let it drop from the spoon in a slow stream. As the slime drops, move the balloon toward it. You might find this easier with the help of a friend or adult.

5 Now watch the dropping slime swing toward the balloon and splat onto it.

6 You can also try moving the balloon toward the slime and stopping it at the point where the stream doesn't actually reach it, but stands out horizontally as a solid.

LET'S INVESTIGATE

This experiment also works with water. Try the investigation with the cornstarch and cooking oil and then with cornstarch and water. Can you work out the difference? Does the cornstarch and oil mixture behave in the same way as the cornstarch and water—in other words, is it a non-Newtonian fluid (see page 10)?

Inside the Science

The balloon becomes charged with static electricity when you rub it on your hair because it picks up extra electrons, which give it a negative charge. Negatively charged molecules attract positive and some neutrally charged molecules. Both the cornstarch particles and water molecules are attracted to the now negatively charged balloon. When the cornstarch particles are in the bowl, there are forces acting on them (including gravity) which are stronger than the weak force of the electrically charged balloon, so they remain in the bowl. When you drip the cornstarch, you create a thin stream of cornstarch particles and water molecules which are light enough to be pulled toward the balloon. Close to the balloon, the water gets pulled out from between the cornstarch particles, so they act as a solid. To learn more about this, see *Basic Cornstarch Slime*, on pages 26–29.

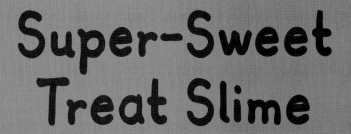

Super-Sweet Treat Slime

When colored in pretty pinks, blues, and yellows, some of the slimes in this book look like ice cream and good enough to eat, but they would taste disgusting and could make you ill. Just once in a while you could make this sweet slime and enjoy a nibble as well as a stretch, a squish, and a squeeze. It would be a fun thing to do at a party. Make sure you wash your hands well before making this slime because you are going to eat it as well as play with it. Remember to brush your teeth afterward, too.

You will need

6½oz (180g) gummy candies (such as Haribo Goldbears)

2–3 tablespoons cornstarch (cornflour)

2–3 tablespoons confectioner's (icing) sugar

Cooking oil, such as sunflower or coconut oil

Microwave-safe bowls and a microwave

Small mixing bowl

Tablespoon

Mixing spoon

Sieve (optional)

Oven mitts (gloves)

Teaspoon

Ziplock bag (optional)

1 Wash your hands with soap and water, and wipe down the work surface so it is really clean. Sort the candies into two or three different piles with similar colors (e.g. green and white together) and put each pile in a different microwave-safe bowl.

2 Mix the cornstarch and confectioner's sugar in the mixing bowl. If the sugar is lumpy, sift it into the bowl so your slime will be nice and smooth.

3 Take the first bowl and ask an adult to help you heat the colored candies in the microwave on full power for 15 seconds. Check to see if the candies have melted. If they haven't, heat them for another 15 seconds and check again. Keep microwaving for a few seconds at a time until they have melted—it doesn't take long. When the candies have melted, use the oven mitts to remove the bowl from the microwave. DO NOT TOUCH the candies because they will be hot.

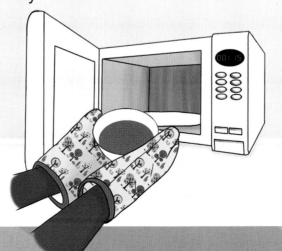

4 Add a teaspoon of the cornstarch mixture to the melted candies and stir. Keep adding the mixture, a little at a time, and stirring, until the slime starts to form a dough.

5 Add a few drops of cooking oil to make the mixture more stretchy, then stir again and leave for a couple of minutes.

6 The mixture should now be cool enough to knead with your hands to make slime. If you haven't added enough cornstarch mixture, you might get into a very sticky mess at this stage, so have plenty of the mixture on the work surface to knead into the slime to get rid of the stickiness. But, remember, the more cornstarch mixture you add, the less stretchy your slime will be.

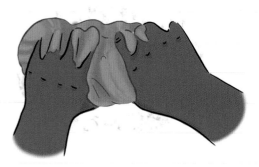

7 Repeat Steps 3 to 6 for the candies in the other colors, and then start sampling your sweet treats!

SAFETY FIRST!

Hot sugar causes bad burns because it sticks to your skin, so be really sure that the mixture has cooled before you touch it—it should be warm, but not hot. Ask an adult to test it for you.

TOP TIPS

Treat slime can get unbelievably sticky, so fill a sink with warm water before you start. Then, if your hands get really gummed up with slime, you can soak them in the water to get them nice and clean again! Soaking the bowls and spoons will help get the sticky goo off them, too!

This slime becomes very firm as it cools down. You can make it stretchy again by sealing it in a Ziplock bag and dropping this into a bowl of hot water for a few minutes to warm up.

Inside the Science

One of the main ingredients in jelly candies is gelatin. Gelatin is made from a protein called collagen which comes from animal bones, skin, and tissues. It is also used in lots of other foods, and many vegetarians try to avoid it. Gelatin melts at a very low temperature—at 95°F (35°C)—which is less than the temperature of the human body. This means it melts in your mouth and makes mousses, marshmallows, and jelly candies extra delicious! It also melts easily in the microwave to make this slime.

LET'S INVESTIGATE

Find out whether the sweet slime can stretch, break, flow, and bounce? Is this slime another example of a non-Newtonian fluid (see page 10), or is it just some tasty goo?

Starburst Slime

If you are a vegetarian, you could try this edible slime because it is made with Starburst candies, which do not contain gelatin. Or have a go at making both this slime and the *Super-Sweet Treat Slime* (see page 80), then you can answer the question: Which makes the best slime? That's difficult as you'll have to decide what makes one better than the other—the taste or the stretchiness! Remember to wash your hands before you begin and brush your teeth after you've had a nibble.

You will need

6oz (165g) bag of Starburst candies

2–3 tablespoons cornstarch (cornflour)

2–3 tablespoons confectioner's (icing) sugar

*

Microwave-safe bowls and a microwave

Small mixing bowl

Tablespoon

Mixing spoon

Sieve (optional)

Oven mitts (gloves)

Ziplock bag

1 Wash your hands with soap and water, and wipe down the work surface so it is really clean. Sort the candies into different colors, unwrap them, and put each color in a different microwave-safe bowl.

2 Mix the cornstarch and confectioner's sugar in the mixing bowl. If the sugar is lumpy, sift it into the bowl so your slime will be lovely and smooth.

3 Take the first bowl and ask an adult to help you heat the colored candies in the microwave on full power for 20 seconds. Stir the candies and then microwave for another 20 seconds. Check to see if the candies have melted. If they haven't, microwave for another 15 seconds. When the candies have melted, use the oven mitts to remove the bowl from the microwave. DO NOT TOUCH the candies—they will be hot!

4 Put a handful of the cornstarch mixture on the work surface and ask an adult to help you tip the melted candies on top. Do not touch the candy goo. Wait for 5 minutes for it to cool down. While you are waiting for the first color to cool down, microwave some of the other candy colors.

5 Ask an adult to check whether the first candy has cooled enough for you to handle it. If it is warm, but not hot, knead it with the cornstarch mix on the countertop, adding more mix if you need to. Pull, stretch, and fold the mixture to trap air inside, as this will make it less sticky and more stretchy.

6 Repeat Steps 3 to 5 for the candies in the other colors, and then have fun twisting the colors together to make beautiful marbled effects.

TOP TIPS

Like the *Super-Sweet Treat Slime* (see page 80), this slime can get unbelievably sticky, so fill your sink with warm water before you begin. If your hands get completely gummed up with slime, just soak them in the sink to get them free! You can also soak your bowls and spoons to get the goo off them!

This slime becomes quite brittle as it cools. To make it stretchy again, seal it in a Ziplock bag and drop this into a bowl of hot water for a few minutes to warm it up.

LET'S INVESTIGATE

As with the *Super-Sweet Treat Slime* (see page 80), investigate these questions: How stretchy is the slime? How does it break? Does it flow? Does it bounce? Compare this slime to the *Super-Sweet Treat Slime* if you have also made that.

Inside the Science

The viscosity of a liquid is a measure of how viscous or runny it is. Water has a very low viscosity, while PVA glue has a much higher viscosity. When you melt the candies in the microwave you turn them into a very viscous liquid. You can then stir in the confectioner's sugar/cornstarch mix, which turns the candy into slime and stops it becoming solid candy again as it cools. Kneading the slime traps air in it. When you play with the candy slime and press on it, the air pressure increases in the bubbles, which stretch the slime around them. The slime is elastic, like a balloon, and wants to spring back. That's what makes the slime stretchy and soft. It will never be as soft as fluffy slime, though, because you are not adding so many bubbles.

You will need

½ cup (120ml) clear PVA glue

2 tablespoons water

½ teaspoon baking soda (bicarbonate of soda)

Blue food coloring

Glitter (optional)

About 1 tablespoon slime activator (eyewash or contact lens solution)

Medium mixing bowl

Measuring cup or pitcher (jug)

Tablespoon

Teaspoon

Mixing spoon

Small cup

Pipette/dropper (optional, but fun)

Something plastic with holes (such as the basket from a salad spinner or a colander)

Long pole (such as a mop)

Ball of strong string

Large tray (to catch the slime)

Blue Waterfall Slime

This is another cool activity that begins with *Transparent Slime* (see page 34). Turn your slime into a slow-motion waterfall—a curtain of hanging drops and the ultimate squiggling worms of slime. You'll find watching it is hypnotic.

1 Make a batch of *Transparent Slime* (see pages 34–37), but this time use blue food coloring and also add some glitter for sparkle (if you wish). The waterfall will flow quicker if you make this slime more stretchy, so take it out of the bowl at an early stage before you start kneading it.

2 Find a way to suspend your holey container high above the tray. Here, we tied string to the container and hung it from a mop balanced between two chairs. Position the tray underneath the container to catch the cascading drops.

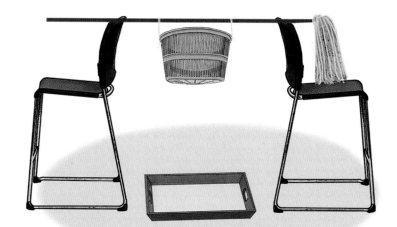

3 Pour the blue slime into the container and wait. You need to be a bit patient here. Watch and wait—and the magic will happen!

LET'S INVESTIGATE

When all the drips of blue slime have reached the tray, ask someone to help you lift the supporting pole and container slowly upward toward the ceiling—how high can you lift the container before the long strands of slime break? Try the slime in different holey containers and time how long it takes for the drops to fall with different sizes or shapes of hole. Does the size or shape of the holes affect the way the strings of slime form?

Inside the Science

Here we see gravity working on the slime. Gravity is pulling down on it gently, so the slime acts like a liquid and flows down, but, because it is very thick (viscous), this is a very slow flow. Around the edges of the holes, the slime is held up by friction with the plastic, but in the center of the hole, away from the plastic, gravity is a stronger force than the attraction that exists between the slime molecules and so the slime drips down. The slime molecules still hold together as they drop, and so the slime forms long strings rather than blobs.

Galaxy Slime Stress Balls

You don't need to be stressed to play with a stress ball, but you could try offering these to adults who are stressed to help them calm down! This project starts off just like *Transparent Slime* (see page 34), so perhaps you could make some stress balls after you've finished playing with a batch of that slime or else make a fresh batch in special colors. One batch of slime should be enough to make two stress balls—you don't want them to be too big—or you could just make half the amount of slime.

You will need

½ cup (120ml) clear PVA glue

2 tablespoons water

½ teaspoon baking soda (bicarbonate of soda)

Food colorings (in 3 colors of your choice)

Glitter

About 1 tablespoon slime activator (eyewash or contact lens solution)

Sparkly stars

2 transparent balloons

 *

Medium mixing bowl

Measuring cup or pitcher (jug)

Tablespoon

Teaspoon

Mixing spoon

3 small bowls or cups

Small cup

Pipette/dropper (optional, but fun)

Plastic drinks bottle

Pointy scissors

1 Pour the PVA glue into the bowl and add the water and baking soda. Stir well until all the water is mixed in. Divide the mixture between three small cups or bowls.

2 Add a little food coloring to each bowl—one very light color and two dark ones work well. Add some glitter to each bowl, too.

3 Pour the activator into the small cup. Use the teaspoon or a pipette/dropper to add a little activator to the first cup or bowl. As you have a smaller amount of glue in each bowl, you will need less activator to bring the mixture together. It will gradually get stringy and begin to come away from the sides of the bowl.

4 Continue adding the activator, a little at a time, until the slime reaches the consistency you want. It is easier to get the slime inside the balloon if it drops well, so take it out and begin kneading it at quite an early stage.

5 When you think the slime is ready, put a few drops of activator on your hands, then pick it up and start stretching and folding it. It might feel a bit sticky at first, but will become soft and stretchy, and lose its stickiness, as you keep working it. Put a little more activator on your hands if it is still a bit sticky. Sprinkle on some sparkly stars and work them into the slime.

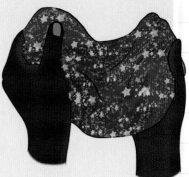

6 Make two more different-colored slimes using the mixtures in the other cups or bowls.

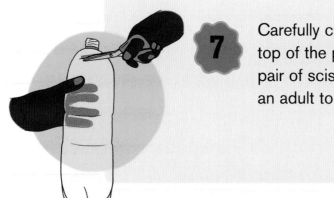

7 Carefully cut the screw section off the top of the plastic bottle with a sharp pair of scissors. You may want to ask an adult to help you with this.

8 Stretch the neck of one of the balloons over the top of the plastic bottle (this will keep the balloon open so you can fill it with slime). Take small pieces of the first slime color and push it into the balloon with your finger. Squeeze the slime down and add some more. This takes patience! When you have a good layer of the first color, add some of the second color. Keep going in this way with different layers of colors until about half of each color is squeezed into the balloon.

9 Push the slime down away from the neck of the balloon, twist the neck to keep the slime down, and tie off the balloon. Repeat for the other balloon.

10 Squish and squeeze the balloons to see the different colors blending and the stars glittering. As you stretch a balloon, by squeezing it, you'll see that it becomes more transparent, enabling you to see the stars and glitter sparkling in the slime more clearly.

LET'S INVESTIGATE

Make a small batch of *Basic Cornstarch Slime* (see pages 26–29) and pour it into another balloon using the plastic bottle top to stretch the neck as before. Pull up the neck of the balloon, then twist and tie it off. Compare how the PVA glue stress ball and the cornstarch ball feel and behave as you squeeze and squash them. Remember to press the cornstarch slime slowly—it will move because it's a liquid. Bang it hard and it's a solid (see page 29). Try bouncing both stress balls, and see what happens.

Inside the Science

If you've made stress balls with both PVA glue slime and cornstarch slime and tried bouncing them, you'll have found that one bounces well and the other doesn't bounce at all. Whether a ball bounces or not depends on how elastic it is. Elastic means that when you squash or stretch it, it tries to go back to its original shape. When the elastic PVA ball hits the ground, it stretches and squashes, and then tries to spring back to its original shape, but, as the ground is in the way, there's no room for this to happen. It is the pushing against the ground as it tries to become round again that makes the ball bounce back up. When the cornstarch ball hits the ground, the water is forced out of the slime, making it hard (see page 29). It is not elastic like the PVA ball and there is no instant spring-back to bounce the ball back into the air. It stays flat!

TOP TIP

Most stress balls are made with two balloons, one over the top of the other, in case one splits. These balls are made with just one transparent balloon, so you can see the colors and sparkles inside. It is best to play with them in the kitchen or backyard— any place where it doesn't matter if the balloon splits and squirts out slime!

Orbeez Volcano

Although not strictly a slime, Orbeez are made of a polymer, like PVA slime, so it seems okay to include them in a slime book. Orbeez are also used in the *Frog Spawn Slime* (see page 104)—if you've made that slime, you'll know what brilliant fun they are. This erupting volcano is awesome—it's just a balloon filled with Orbeez that erupts when you cut off the top!

You will need

Transparent balloon

Orbeez in any color
(1,000 or more—
available online)

*

Plastic drinks bottle

Sharp, pointy scissors

Balloon pump
(optional)

Large mixing bowl

Large tray

1 First make a funnel with the plastic bottle. Remove the cap and ask an adult to help you use a pair of sharp scissors to cut around the bottle, about 3in. (7.5cm) down from the neck.

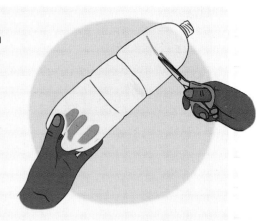

2 Inflate the balloon with air a few times, so it is well stretched, and then let the air go.

3 Push the neck of the balloon over the neck of the plastic bottle, then use the bottle as a funnel to pour about a heaped tablespoon of Orbeez into the balloon.

SAFETY FIRST!

Although Orbeez are not toxic, they should not be eaten. Small children might think they are candies (sweets), so be careful with them. When you have finished playing with your Orbeez, don't throw them down the sink or toilet as they can block drains. Either put them in the trash can (rubbish bin) or dig them into your plant pots or flowerbeds where they will help keep your plants moist.

4 You will need someone to help you with the next part. Stretch the neck of the balloon over a faucet (tap). Ask your helper to support the balloon underneath (it will get quite heavy), then turn on the faucet and fill the balloon with water until it has stretched to a diameter of about 5in. (13cm). With your helper still supporting the balloon, squeeze the top closed with your fingers and ease it off the faucet—you could well get wet at this point! Then carefully tie off the balloon.

5 This is the hardest part—you have to wait! Leave the balloon overnight to allow the Orbeez to absorb the water and reach their full size. After this time, the Orbeez will have filled the balloon and stretched the sides. The balloon has now turned into an Orbeez stress ball. Have fun with the ball—squish it, squelch it, squeeze it, but try not to burst it!

6 Now prepare for the volcano. This part is best done outside. Place the mixing bowl on the large tray to catch any flying Orbeez. Put your balloon in the bowl and pull the neck up so it is stretched. Cut the balloon close to the Orbeez, then stand back and watch the eruption! Afterward you will still have all the Orbeez to play with.

LET'S INVESTIGATE

If you have enough Orbeez and another balloon, try putting more Orbeez in the balloon, but use the same amount of water—just keep adding water until the balloon is the same size as before. There will be enough to expand the Orbeez. Does using more Orbeez make for a better eruption? How would you tell if it was better? You would have to measure something—the height the Orbeez jumped to, how long they kept spilling out, how far they scattered…

Inside the Science

You can learn more about the science behind Orbeez if you make some *Frog Spawn Slime* (see pages 104–105), but why do the Orbeez in the volcano explode out? Balloons are made from elastic polymers, either natural latex or a man-made rubber. When you inflate the balloon with air, or with water and Orbeez, it stretches, but it is trying to pull back to its original size all the time. The balloon can't do this while tied up, but as soon as you cut it, it shrinks back again, squeezing out the Orbeez and any water that hasn't been absorbed.

Orbeez are fascinating. Although they are often used as toys, you also find them under the greens on golf courses where they slowly release their water. This makes them perfect for keeping the grass moist. The same polymer is used in diapers (nappies) to absorb wee!

Slimes Inspired by Nature

Slime Gallery

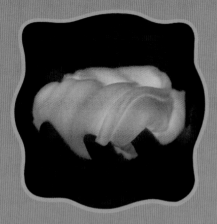

102
Glow-in-the-Dark Ectoplasm

Find out about photoluminescence—that's the longest word in the book!

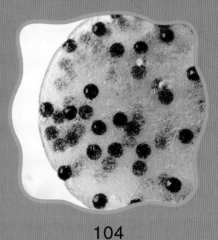

104
Frog Spawn Slime

Learn about the incredible polymer in Orbeez.

106
Stretchy Salt Dough

Discover gluten and find out how it helps bread rise.

110
Natural Chia Seed Slime

All about mucilage—an amazing natural slime.

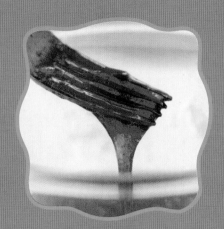

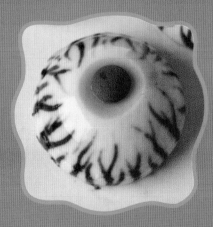

You will need

½ cup (120ml) clear PVA glue

2 tablespoons water

½ teaspoon baking soda (bicarbonate of soda)

1–2 tablespoons green glow-in-the-dark craft paint

About 1 tablespoon slime activator (eyewash or contact lens solution)

Medium mixing bowl

Measuring cup or pitcher (jug)

Tablespoon

Teaspoon

Mixing spoon

Small cup

Pipette/dropper (optional, but fun)

Ziplock bag

Glow-in-the-Dark Ectoplasm

Anyone who enjoys spooky movies knows that ectoplasm is the gooey slime produced by ghosts! If you are having a Hallowe'en party, then glow-in-the-dark ectoplasm will really spook your friends!

1 Follow the method on pages 34–37 to make a batch of *Transparent Slime*, but this time don't add anything but green glow-in-the-dark craft paint. Ectoplasm should be nice and stretchy, and not too firm, so be careful when adding the activator, as too much will make the slime too stiff.

2 If you would like your ectoplasm to be completely transparent, leave it inside a Ziplock bag for a few days to allow the bubbles to clear (see page 37).

FASCINATING FACT

There are many glow-in-the-dark creatures, such as fireflies and some species of fish. Sometimes the sea itself seems to glow because it contains so many bioluminescent micro-organisms (microscopic plants and animals). Bioluminescent means that an animal or plant can produce its own light.

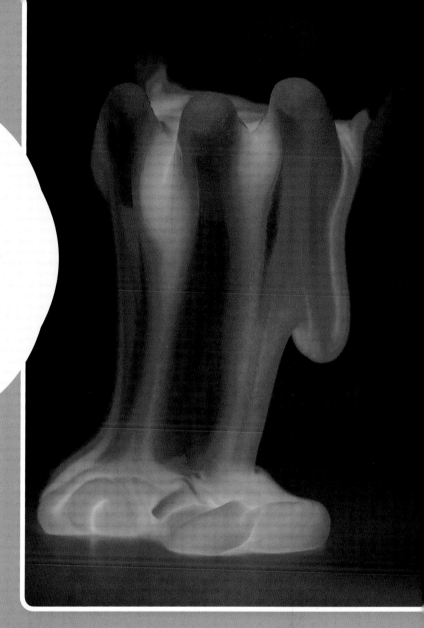

LET'S INVESTIGATE

Divide your ectoplasm into two and put each half in a separate Ziplock bag. Put one bag in a dark cabinet and the other half on a light windowsill. Leave the bags all day. When it goes dark, take the bags into a dark room. Which bag glows the brightest?

Inside the Science

The glow-in-the-dark paint is photoluminescent. The paint glows because it contains chemicals called phosphors, which store energy when they are left in a light place and then release it, as light, for quite a long time. You need to energize the phosphors in the paint by leaving it in light before they will glow and then they slowly release their stored energy. Toy manufacturers work to find phosphors that can be energized by normal light and which will glow for as long as possible.

Frog Spawn Slime

Black Orbeez
(available online)

½ cup (120ml) clear
PVA glue

2 tablespoons water

½ teaspoon baking
soda (bicarbonate
of soda)

About 1 tablespoon
slime activator
(eyewash or contact
lens solution)

Large glass

Tablespoon

Teaspoon

Medium mixing bowl

Measuring cup or
pitcher (jug)

Mixing spoon

Small cup

Pipette/dropper
(optional, but fun)

Sieve

Frog spawn is a natural slime. When a frog lays eggs they sink to the bottom of the pond, but the jelly around them absorbs water (just like Orbeez do) and they float up to the surface. The jelly protects the eggs as they grow into tadpoles. It's fun to trick your friends with this fake frog spawn. To make it, you will need black Orbeez (you may have to buy them online). They are a magical material and amazing to play with, even before you add them to slime.

1 First prepare your Orbeez. Fill the glass with water, tip in a teaspoon of Orbeez, and watch them grow! Don't let them get too big or they won't look like frogs' eggs—just take them out of the glass of water to stop them growing.

2 Now for the slime. Make a batch of *Transparent Slime* (see pages 34–37), but don't add any food coloring, glitter, or add-ins—frog spawn slime needs to be nice and clear. If you want the slime to be really clear, you will have to make it a few days before you need it to allow the bubbles to disappear (see page 37).

3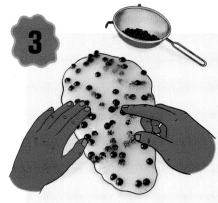

Use the sieve to drain the Orbeez, then add some to the slime and mix them in. At first, the Orbeez will keep popping out of the slime. If you leave them for a while, they will absorb water from the slime and get bigger and more rubbery. Soon they will begin to feel as if they are just part of the slime.

4 Gather the frog spawn slime together and it makes a great bouncy ball!

5 Leave the other Orbeez in the glass of water to grow to their full size and then play with them, too. They are amazingly bouncy!

Inside the Science

Orbeez are made from another polymer (see page 8). All slimes are just water held together with a net of polymer chains. The polymer in Orbeez (called sodium polacrylate) is much better at holding onto water than other polymers, so, when they are in water, the Orbeez balls grow to 100–300 times their original size. The slime inside them is also much stiffer than PVA slime because there are more cross-links and these are stronger. Try crushing one with your finger to feel how different the slime is.

LET'S INVESTIGATE

How much can Orbeez expand? Measure the diameter of one before and after you have soaked it in water. Do the math. How many times bigger has it become? Bounce one of the balls that you left to soak in the glass. How high will it bounce? How many times will the ball bounce when you drop it?

Stretchy Salt Dough

This isn't really a true slime, but the science behind it focuses on a slime that helps to make one of our favorite foods—bread. When you have made your salt dough, have fun modeling and molding it before "cooking" it in the microwave. This helps the salt dough to dry out quickly so that, finally, you can paint your artistic creations.

You will need

2 cups (250g) all-purpose (plain) flour

1 cup (280g) table salt

1 cup (240ml) lukewarm water

Large mixing bowl

Measuring cup or pitcher (jug)

Mixing spoon

Paper towel

Large microwave-safe plate

Microwave

Oven mitts (gloves)

Paints and a paintbrush

1 Stir the flour and salt together in the bowl until they are well mixed.

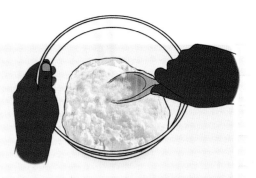

2 Gradually pour the water into the bowl, stirring well each time you add a bit. Keep adding the water and stirring until the mixture starts to come together to form a lumpy dough.

3 Get your hands in and start bringing the dough together into a ball. If the dough is too crumbly, then add a little more water. If it's too sticky, add a little more flour.

4 Turn the dough out onto the countertop and begin kneading it. Squash it, fold it, stretch it, and thump it. The longer and more firmly you knead the dough, the smoother and stretchier it will become.

5 Once you have a smooth, stretchy dough, start making your models—you can be as imaginative as you like here!

6 Put a piece of paper towel on the large plate and carefully place your models on that. Ask an adult to help you to dry your models in the microwave on full power for 10 seconds at a time. After each 10-second burst, check to see if the models are dry. Do not microwave the models for longer bursts, or they will burn. Remember, smaller, thinner models will dry more quickly than larger, thicker ones.

7 Once your models are dry, use oven mitts to remove the plate from the microwave and let them cool completely before you paint them.

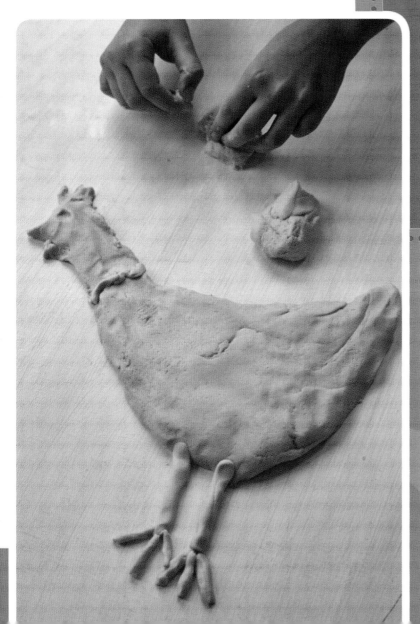

Inside the Science

Flour contains two proteins called glutenin and gliadin. Gliadin's long molecules are curled up into balls, while glutenin's molecules make long, sprawling tangles. When you add water to flour, these proteins unfold and begin to bond together. As you knead dough you stretch out the proteins and more and more bonds are formed until they make a stretchy protein sheet called gluten. This is the "slime" in bread and, like PVA slime, you can blow bubbles in it (see page 62). In bread, the gluten traps bubbles of gas, which make it rise. In salt dough, the gluten makes the dough smooth and elastic, which is why it is so good for making models.

LET'S INVESTIGATE

When making salt dough, try stretching it before you knead it, then stretch it again after one minute of kneading, then after two minutes of kneading, etc. Can you feel a difference in stretchiness each time? How long can you keep kneading the dough for—it's hard work!

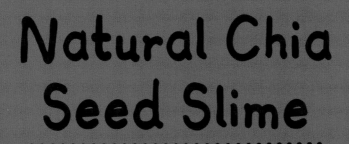

Natural Chia Seed Slime

This is a great slime to make if you don't want to use borax-based activators. It uses the natural slime that forms around some types of seeds when you soak them in water. You'll discover that chia seed slime feels very different to normal PVA slimes because the seeds make it rough. You can buy chia seeds and xanthan gum in health food stores and some grocery stores.

You will need

2 tablespoons chia seeds

1 cup (240ml) water

Food coloring (in a color of your choice)

1 teaspoon xanthan gum

2–3 cups (240–360g) cornstarch (cornflour)

*

Airtight plastic container

Tablespoon

Measuring cup or pitcher (jug)

Mixing spoon

Large mixing bowl

Teaspoon

1 Put the chia seeds in the container and pour in the water.

2 Stir well, put the lid on the container, and place in the fridge overnight. It's a good idea to stir the seeds after a couple of hours to stop them clumping together.

3 In the morning, you'll discover that the seeds have gone all slimy. Enjoy plunging your hands into the seeds and squeezing, squelching, and letting the mixture run through your fingers. Break up any clumps as you do this.

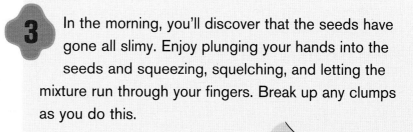

4 Now tip the slimy seeds into the mixing bowl and add a little food coloring and the xanthan gum. Stir everything well, but don't worry if the gum doesn't mix in completely. The color won't show much at this stage because the chia seeds are dark—so don't add too much food coloring!

5 Start mixing the cornstarch into the chia seeds. Keep adding more cornstarch until the slime loses its stickiness.

6 Use your hands after the slime has started to come together and knead it well. If the slime becomes crumbly, then knead in a teaspoon of water at a time until it becomes stretchy again.

LET'S INVESTIGATE

* How does this slime compare to the cornstarch putties made with just two ingredients in the *Cornstarch Challenge* (see pages 56–57)? Is this slime more like those putties or the PVA-based slimes? Try out the various tests you did with the putties and slimes to work out which is the stretchiest and the bounciest, or which one flows best.

* You could also try making slime by mixing 1 teaspoon of xanthan gum into ½ cup (120ml) of water and then just adding cornstarch. What difference do the chia seeds make to this slime (apart from making it feel rough to the touch)?

TOP TIP

This slime is made with natural products and will go moldy, so keep it in a sealed container in the fridge and throw it away after a week. If the slime dries out, knead a little more water into it.

Inside the Science

Chia seeds contain large amounts of a substance called mucilage. When you soak mucilage in water, it swells up, absorbing up to 27 times its weight in water and turning into the jelly you saw around the seeds when you made your chia slime. In nature, this jelly forms around the seeds as they germinate (begin to grow) in the soil, keeping them moist. Mucilage is a natural polymer, this time a polysaccharide or long chain of sugar molecules. The starches in cornstarch, flour, and potatoes are other examples of polysaccharides. Mucilage makes slime by holding onto water molecules in the same way as slimes made with PVA glue.

Fake Snot

Humans produce a lot of slime—if you have a baby brother or sister with a cold, you can see just how much slime comes down their noses. It may be disgusting, but slime is important to protect us from disease. Try making this fake snot to gross out your friends!

You will need

½ cup (120ml) water

3 packets unflavored gelatin

4 tablespoons corn (golden) syrup

Green food coloring (optional)

Kettle

Measuring cup or pitcher (jug)

2 small bowls

Fork

1 Ask an adult to help you heat some water in a kettle until it is very hot, but not quite boiling. Pour ½ cup (120ml) of the not-quite-boiling water into one of the bowls and sprinkle in the gelatin. Use a fork to stir in the powder and let soften for 5 minutes.

2 Pour the corn syrup into the other bowl.

3 Stir the gelatin mix with the fork until all the lumps have gone and then slowly add it to the corn syrup until the mixture looks like snot. Use the fork to stir the mixture, as this will pull out long strands of snot. Add a little green food coloring if you want to make the slime even more disgusting.

FASCINATING FACT

Your body is wrapped in skin to keep out pathogens (microscopic organisms such as viruses and bacteria which can make you ill). However, there have to be openings so that you can breathe, eat, hear, see, wee, and poop. Each of these openings is like a doorway, which the pathogens can get through, so they need to be defended. Snot or mucus, a slimy, antibacterial liquid, protects your nose. There are also lots of tiny hairs in your nose that trap dust and pathogens. When snot runs down your nose, it picks up these nasties and they end up on a tissue when you blow your nose—or on your hand if you sneeze into it!

Inside the Science

This slime looks like snot because it is made of the same ingredients—protein, sugar, and water. Although these are different types of protein and sugar, snot has a very similar makeup. The gelatin in fake snot is made up of long protein molecules. When you mix it with water, the water molecules cross-link with the gelatin to make a mesh. (The water mustn't be too hot or it can't form bonds with the protein.) The corn syrup contains sugar. This structure can combine with and hold a lot of water. Snot is mostly water and so is fake snot.

Bio-Plastic

There is too much plastic in the world and it is polluting our oceans. What we need is biodegradable plastic. This is plastic that rots away and doesn't stick around for hundreds of years. Scientists are working hard to make plastics like these. The one shown here is a very simple plastic that will biodegrade—it's not strong enough to wrap up food, but you can stretch and mold it.

You will need

2 tablespoons cornstarch (cornflour)

3 tablespoons water

½ teaspoon cooking oil

Food coloring (optional)

Microwave-safe bowl and a microwave

Tablespoon

Teaspoon

Mixing spoon

Oven mitts (gloves)

Cookie cutters (optional)

1 Mix the cornstarch, water, and cooking oil in the bowl to make a milky-looking liquid. Add a little food coloring if you would like colored plastic.

2 Ask an adult to help you heat the mixture in the microwave on a high setting for about 50 seconds. The mixture should begin to bubble and become translucent. That means it is partly see-through, like baking parchment.

3 Use the oven mitts to remove the bowl from the microwave and let the mixture cool down.

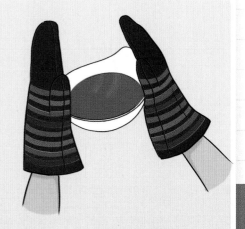

4 Once the mixture has cooled down, knead it until it is smooth and soft. You will now be able to mold it or cut it into different shapes with cookie cutters. Let the molded biodegradable plastic harden for about 24 hours.

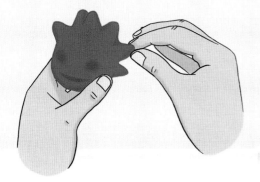

Inside the Science

When you first stir the cornstarch and water together to make the plastic, they mix but the molecules remain quite separate. The starch molecules are already polymers—long chains of repeated patterns—but they are all wrapped up like a ball of string. When you heat anything, you give it energy, which makes the molecules inside move faster. So, when you heat the cornstarch mix, the starch molecules move more and more until they unravel into long strings, which then get tangled up with all the other strings nearby. They also get tangled up with the water molecules, which can't escape from them. That's your plastic.

LET'S INVESTIGATE

When something biodegrades, it means that microorganisms (living things such as bacteria that are too small to be seen without a microscope) eat away at it until it becomes part of the soil and air again. Is your plastic biodegradable? To find out, try burying some in a plant pot in your backyard and see what happens to it. Remember to keep the soil moist because microorganisms are living things and need water to survive. Dig the plastic up after a couple of weeks and see what has happened to it. If it hasn't changed much, leave it for longer and look again.

Plastic Milk

Plastic made from milk! Can you believe it? This isn't quite the same as the other slimes in the book because it isn't as stretchy or as good to play with. But you can mold it and then it dries into a hard plastic that can be painted. It's great for making Christmas decorations, and, like *Bio-Plastic* (see page 116), it is biodegradable.

You will need

2 cups (480ml) whole milk

8 teaspoons white vinegar

Microwave-safe bowl and a microwave

Measuring cup or pitcher (jug)

Oven mitts (gloves)

Teaspoon

Wooden mixing spoon

Sieve

Mixing bowl

Paper towels

Small cookie cutters (the ones with plungers are best)

Paints and a fine paintbrush

1 Pour the milk into the bowl and ask an adult to help you heat it up in the microwave until it is hot, but not boiling. Use oven mitts to remove the bowl from the microwave.

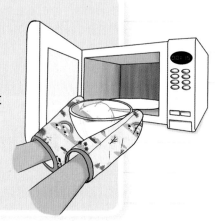

2 Add the vinegar to the milk and stir for a few seconds. The milk will change, becoming full of small white lumps called curds.

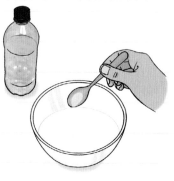

3 Strain the milk through the sieve over the sink or into another bowl. The curds will be caught in the sieve. Wait a few moments for all the liquid to drain through.

4 Rinse the curds in the sieve under the faucet (tap), then tip them onto several layers of paper towel and squeeze out more of the liquid.

5 Pull the curds together to form a lump and knead this until it is smooth. This is your plastic milk.

6 Shape the plastic milk into a thin disc on the countertop and use cookie cutters to cut out different shapes. Leave the shapes to dry out and harden for a few days before painting them.

Inside the Science

Scientists describe things as plastic if they can be molded into another shape, but most people now use the word to describe the material used to make millions of things, from bags to containers and chairs to keyboards. In the early 20th century, milk plastic was used to make all kinds of things like buttons and combs. Plastics are always polymers. Remember a polymer is a chain of repeating molecules (see page 8). Milk contains a protein called casein, which is a long molecule that's curled up into a tight ball. When you add vinegar (which is an acid) to hot milk, the casein unfolds and reorganizes itself into long chains—it becomes a polymer, which can be molded into shapes. In the past, people added a chemical called formaldehyde to cross-link the milk polymer and make it stiffer and stronger.

LET'S INVESTIGATE

Vinegar is an acid. Do you get the same effect if you make the plastic milk with another acid such as lemon juice? What if the milk is cold when you add the vinegar? Does more vinegar result in better plastic?

Jelly Eyeballs

Is jelly a slime? That's a question you can ask yourself after you've made these gruesome jelly eyeballs, which you can pop in your mouth to horrify your friends. This recipe makes much more jelly than you need for the eyeballs, so pour what is left into molds and then find out how slime-like jelly is— or you could just eat it for dessert!

You will need

Packet of green or blue jello (jelly)

Green or blue food coloring

Red food coloring

Water

8 teaspoons gelatin powder

14oz (400g) can of condensed milk

Small chocolate drops

 *

Kettle

Pipette/dropper

Spherical ice cube mold (with 6 spheres)

Measuring cup or pitcher (jug)

2 medium mixing bowls

Small mixing bowl

Wooden spoon

Sieve

Jello (jelly) molds or pudding basins (optional)

Toothpick

1 Ask an adult to help you boil some water in a kettle and make some green or blue jello (jelly) in one of the medium bowls, following the directions on the packet. Add some food coloring to make the colors deeper. If you want brown eyes, add red food coloring to green jello. Let the jello cool to room temperature.

2 Use a clean pipette/dropper to put a little colored jello at the bottom of each spherical mold to make the colored iris of the eyes. Put the molds in the fridge carefully.

3 To make the white jelly for the eyes, pour ½ cup (120ml) of cold water into the small bowl. Sprinkle the gelatin on top of the cold water and leave for 5 minutes.

4 Open the can of condensed milk and pour it into the other medium bowl.

5 Ask an adult to help you boil the kettle again and add 1 cup (240ml) of boiling water to the condensed milk. Mix well with the wooden spoon.

6 Add the gelatin—which will have swollen up—and water in the small bowl to the condensed milk and mix this in really well until there are no lumps. Add another ½ cup (120ml) of boiling water and mix again. Let cool to room temperature.

7 Use the sieve to strain the white jelly mixture into the measuring cup or pitcher in order to take out any lumps.

8 Check to see if the colored jello in the molds has set, then carefully spoon in the white jelly mixture, filling right up to the top of the half-molds.

TOP TIP

The eyeballs will not set unless they are cooled in the fridge. Cover the remaining jello and leave it in a cool place (but not as cold as the fridge) while your first eyeballs are setting and then you can use the molds to make a second batch of eyeballs.

9 Put the upper part of the spherical molds on top and continue filling up the "eyeballs" through the holes in the top. Some molds come with tiny funnels to help you do this. Return the molds to the fridge and let the eyeballs set for several hours.

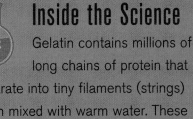

Inside the Science

Gelatin contains millions of long chains of protein that separate into tiny filaments (strings) when mixed with warm water. These proteins are *hydrophyllic* ("water-loving"), so each string attracts water molecules (see page 45). This means there are fewer molecules free to flow through the mixture. As the mixture cools, the water-rich strings begin to bump into each other and become tangled. The remaining water gets caught up in this tangle of protein filaments and the mixture becomes a gel. Jellies are neither solids nor liquids. The proteins are solid, but the water is liquid.

10 Either keep the rest of the colored and white jellos out of the fridge to make more eyeballs (see *Top Tip*), or pour them into jello molds or pudding basins and refrigerate, so you can eat them later for dessert.

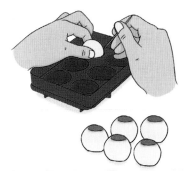

11 When the eyeballs have set completely, gently ease them out of the molds—use the toothpick to loosen them if you need to.

12 Place a chocolate drop on top of each colored iris—these are the pupils of the eyes. Use the end of the toothpick and red food coloring to paint on some ghoulish red veins.

Further Reading

The Science of Slime (see pages 8–13) and the *Inside the Science* panels for each project are just snippets of information about the science involved in slime. If you would like to find out more, take a look at these websites and videos, almost all of which have been designed for kids.

Atoms and molecules

- https://www.ducksters.com/science/the_atom.php
- https://www.ducksters.com/science/molecules.php
- http://www.chem4kids.com/files/atom_intro.html
- https://www.khanacademy.org/partner-content/mit-k12/mit-k12-materials/v/atoms-and-molecules
- https://ed.ted.com/lessons/what-is-the-shape-of-a-molecule-george-zaidan-and-charles-morton

Balls bounce–why?

- https://www.exploratorium.edu/sports/ball_bounces/ballbounces2.html

Bio-plastics

- https://www.explainthatstuff.com/bioplastics.html
- http://tiki.oneworld.org/plastic/plastic.html

Color and light

- https://www.youtube.com/watch?v=UZ5UGnU7oOI
- https://www.sciencelearn.org.nz/resources/47-colours-of-light
- https://www.ducksters.com/science/light_spectrum.php

Elements and the Periodic Table

- https://www.ducksters.com/science/elements.php

Floating and sinking

- http://mocomi.com/floatation-and-relative-density/
- http://mocomi.com/buoyancy/
- http://mocomi.com/floating-egg/

Frog spawn

- https://www.topmarks.co.uk/Spring/TadpolesHatch.aspx?age=ks2
- http://www.countryfile.com/blog-post/top-facts-about-frog-spawn
- http://www.froglife.org/

Gelatin

- https://www.cnet.com/news/appliance-science-the-firm-chemistry-of-gelatin/

Hagfish and other animal slimes

- https://www.popsci.com/animal-goo#page-4

How eyes work

- https://kidshealth.org/en/kids/eyes.html
- www.youtube.com/watch?v=syaQgmxb5i0

Magnetite

- https://uwaterloo.ca/earth-sciences-museum/resources/just-kids/minerals-kids#Magnetite

Mucus (snot)

- https://ed.ted.com/lessons/how-mucus-keeps-us-healthy-katharina-ribbeck#watch

Nebulae

- https://www.spacetelescope.org/images/archive/category/nebulae/
- https://kidsastronomy.com/the-universe/nebulae/

Non-Newtonian fluids

- https://www.sciencelearn.org.nz/resources/1502-non-newtonian-fluids
- https://vimeo.com/187080001
- https://ed.ted.com/lessons/why-is-ketchup-so-hard-to-pour-george-zaidan

Photoluminescence

- https://www.explainthatstuff.com/luminescence.html

Polymers

- https://pslc.ws/macrog/kidsmac/wiap.htm
- https://kids.kiddle.co/Polymer
- http://www.sciencekidsathome.com/science_topics/amazing-polymers.html

Polymer in Orbeez and diapers (nappies)

- https://www.encyclopedia.com/science/academic-and-educational-journals/sodium-polyacrylate (This one is a bit complicated.)

Rubber balloons

- https://www.explainthatstuff.com/rubber.html

Static electricity

- https://www.ducksters.com/science/static_electricity.php
- http://thekidshouldseethis.com/post/the-science-of-static-electricity-ted-ed

Transparent, translucent, and opaque

- http://science.jrank.org/pages/1593/Color-Transparent-translucent-opaque.html

Xanthan gum

- https://wiki.kidzsearch.com/wiki/Xanthan_gum

Index

Borax-free slimes

If you don't want to use borax in your slime, then choose one of these fantastic recipes, which are made with other ingredients.

Acknowledgment

To Rob Carter MSci (Chemistry) for checking the science and ensuring that, although it is simple, it isn't wrong.